The

NECRONOMNOMNOM

The NECRONOMNOMNOM

RECIPES AND RITES FROM THE LORE OF

H. P. LOVECRAFT

MIKE SLATER

Edited by Thomas Roache
Illustrations by Kurt Komoda

The Countryman Press
A division of W. W. Norton & Company
Independent Publishers Since 1923

Copyright © 2019 by Red Duke Games, LLC

For information about permission to reproduce selections from this book, write to Permissions, The Countryman Press, 500 Fifth Avenue, New York, NY 10110

For information about special discounts for bulk purchases, please contact W. W. Norton Special Sales at specialsales@wwnorton.com or 800-233-4830

Library of Congress Cataloging-in-Publication Data

Names: Slater, Mike, author. | Roache, Thomas, editor. | Komoda, Kurt, illustrator.
Title: The Necronomnomnom : recipes and rites from the lore of H. P. Lovecraft / Mike Slater, edited by Thomas Roache ; illustrations by Kurt Komoda.
Identifiers: LCCN 2019030377 | ISBN 9781682684382 (cloth) | ISBN 9781682684399 (epub)
Subjects: LCSH: Cooking. | LCGFT: Cookbooks.
Classification: LCC TX714 .S586168 2019 | DDC 641.5—dc23
LC record available at https://lccn.loc.gov/2019030377

Manufacturing by ToppanLeefung
Book design by Faceout Studio, Paul Nielsen
Production manager: Devon Zahn

The Countryman Press
www.countrymanpress.com

A division of W. W. Norton & Company, Inc.
500 Fifth Avenue, New York, NY 10110
www.wwnorton.com

10 9 8 7 6 5 4 3

OCTOBER 2021

I dedicate this to my parents—because they always supported me, even if they didn't necessarily understand what interested me.

I dedicate this to my beautiful, supportive family to whom I couldn't be more dedicated.

I dedicate this to the scholars who came before me—real and unreal.

I dedicate this to the folks who believed so hard that this book became real.

But most of all, I dedicate this book to my buddy Tom, because without his boundless energy and ability to trust my crazy ideas, this book would not exist. May this book nourish your body, soul (if you still have one), and sense of humor. It's been a wonderful journey.

—Mike Slater (The Five O'Clock Shadow Out of Time)
October 2019

Thanks to all my family who loves me for who I am. I dedicate this to them, who I hope know how much I truly love them.

Thanks to Mike, my true friend, who can make a great joke turn into an idea I can run with, then trip over, fall on my face with, get creative on, lose then find again, juggle with, cook up and take pictures of, and ultimately spin gold with. Thanks for making "this" worthwhile.

To whoever reads this: Everything happens for a reason (a quote that my mom gave me at an early age that I believe with all my heart). I also believe that ideas and experiences have weight and power. It is up to you to do what you will with them. But, if you follow your ideas and learn from your experiences, you will have reasons for the good things that happen in your life.

—Thomas R. Roache, PE (The Disembodied Voice)
October 2019

"The most merciful thing in the world, I think, is the ability of the human stomach to correlate all its contents . . . Someday the cooking together of dissociated recipes will open up such terrifying platters of comestibles, and of our frightful position before them, that we shall either go mad from their ingestion or flee from the table into the pizza and savories of the Packaged Food Age."

—(apologies to) H. P. Lovecraft

I have come into possession of a most singular tome. The circumstances of its arrival are beyond strange, as it is an aged book of strange and fascinating recipes —but as my wife will tell anyone within hearing, I am no cook. I must keep it concealed from her, for I fear that her adventurous nature would dispose her to try to bring these dire dishes to fruition —and I am not at all certain that would be wise. There is evidence that others before have tried and I shudder at the hints I have uncovered as to their fates. Such work requires insightful interpretation, research, and experimentation. I must proceed cautiously. Not all is as it seems with this volume . . .

CONTENTS

Soups and Salads

Main Dishes

Sides

Breakfast

Children's Meals

Desserts

FOREWORD AND FOREWARNINGS

The tome you hold in you hands or other manipulatory appendages derives from an older codex. Attempts were made to civilize it. Niceties were added: tables of content, appendices, measures and servings (but . . . serving what?). They seem to have held. No more of the editing staff have mysteriously vanished, though the sanity of some may have . . . suffered. Be warned: If cooking is a science, eldritch cooking is alchemy, prayer, and sacrifice!

We have tested these versions of the terrifying dishes found in these pages. The probability of summoning a faceless elder being from beyond Time and Space is much smaller, you'll be comforted to know. Your stove is far less likely to be replaced by a yawning black portal to the Dimension of Unending Wimpering.

All of this came at a cost. This is not a tome for the faint of hearth. You will be called upon still to make your best guess, to experiment, to strive and curse and rail against the forces of Unnature who laugh at our quaint and specific conventions of the kitchen. Be glad for the civilizing influence exerted by the intrepid cadre of chefs and sleuths who have tried to protect your sanity. Most of you can rest easy in the knowledge that this is and shall be all in good fun. Most of you.

A Word About Specific Diets

We neither accept nor reject any mortal food religion. *The Necronomnomnom* serves the will of the Great Old Ones—and they shall consume all. You are, of course, free to remove, add, or substitute anything you find objectionable. We're sure the uncaring ancient entities from whom these rites flow won't mind, and it'll all be perfectly safe. May Vega shine brightly on your efforts.

Auditory Hallucinations

Most of this book was composed to Cryo Chamber and its collection of Lovecraftian collaboration albums. I don't know if you can cook to it, but it sure helped put in whatever you call the frame of mind necessary to covert perfectly good recipes into Lovecraftian horrors from beyond the furthest kitchens of night . . .

DRINKS

MARTINI: SHAKEN, NOT HASTUR

Serves 1, but invoke it not thrice—at peril of your very consciousness

What Must Be Offered

Wasabi sauce from the Men of Kikko

4 ounces soul-shatteringly cold Reyka vodka

4 ounces ~~dried voormis~~ dry vermouth

One Spanish olive

A most singular tome. Beyond strange.

Who would bring these dire dishes to fruition? Evidence others have tried. Hints of their fates cause me to shudder.

Summoning the Unspeakable Martini

Prepare a large glass: bless it with the touch of a thin tendril of wasabi. Do not completely encircle the rim, as this will allow revelers to imbibe as much or as little of the garnish as they wish. Chill the glass.

Under chill Aldebaran, by the shore of the Lake of Hali (ideally), combine the two spirits. The vessel must be strong enough to contain the inevitable clash between the two. Shake violently, and strain.

Once the conflict subsides, pour the conjoined spirits into the large, chilled, and prepared glass of the traditional geometry.

After pouring carefully to avoid washing the garnish into the glass, add a small Spanish olive without pimento for the look of mindless cosmic horror, or with pimento if you prefer the abyss staring back.

must be read carefully, the pages scoured for clues

No simple manual for this—

Sigil of Hastur, from Mr. Ashmore's journal, Jan 1923

Saw a variation of this sigil in the Cranbury records. Origin unknown.

Sigil of Hali T. Carl, 1891

probably the same symbol?

The sigil in Ashmore's journal was a rubbing from something, but he did not say what.

I fear the processes and rituals are partially obscured for reasons I dare not think too deeply on—

The olive **IS** empty. Sometimes

Are there two? Do they move... between?
There's a bond here
can't see it
Can't see it! Damn my eyes!

The Daruma —
The painting of one eye is the setting of a goal. The second eye is painted when the goal is completed

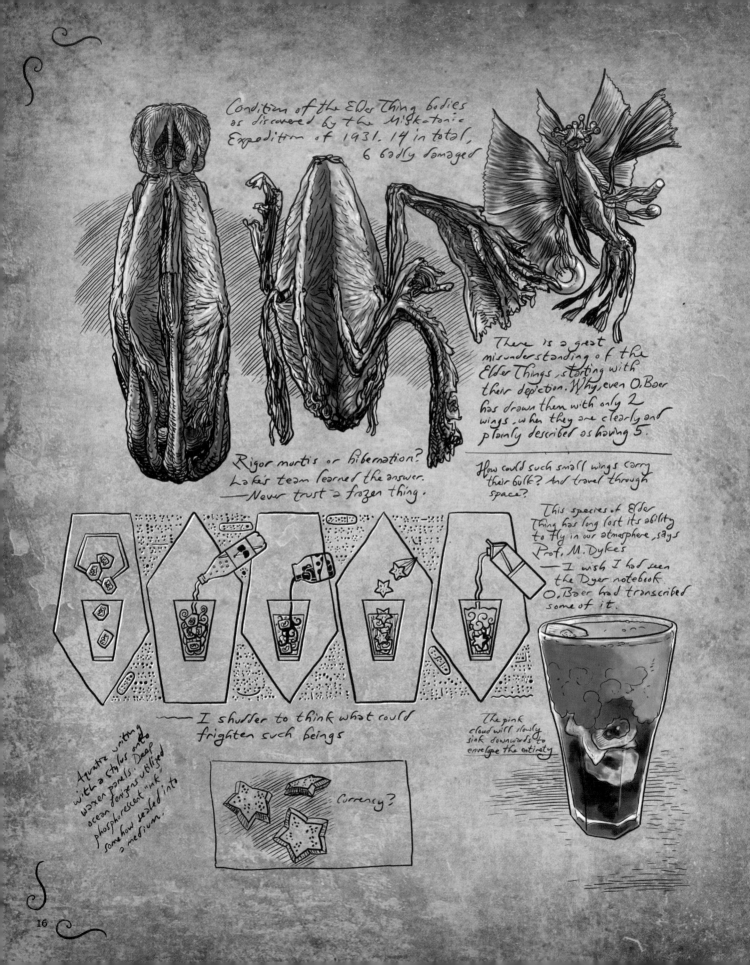

Condition of the Elder Thing bodies as discovered by the Miskatonic Expedition of 1931. 14 in total, 6 badly damaged

There is a great misunderstanding of the Elder Things, starting with their depiction. Why, even O. Baer has drawn them with only 2 wings when they are clearly and plainly described as having 5.

Rigor mortis or hibernation? Lake's team learned the answer. —Never trust a frozen thing.

How could such small wings carry their bulk? And travel through space?

This species of Elder Thing has long lost its ability to fly in our atmosphere, says Prof. M. Dykes —I wish I had seen the Dyer notebook O. Baer had transcribed some of it.

— I shudder to think what could frighten such beings

Aquatic writing with a stylus onto waxen panels. Deaf ocean denizens utilized phosphorescent "ink" somehow sealed into a medium.

Currency?

The pink cloud will slowly sink downwards to envelope the entirety

AT THE FOUNTAINS OF MADNESS

 Serves 1

Provisions

3 to 6 Ursus-Gao-mai encased in ice

10 ounces carbonic tincture of Black Cherry

2 ounces Scarlet Syrup of Maraschin-Yoh

1 ounce half-and-half

Additional Ursus-Gao-mai or similar confections

Preparation

Freeze the creatures and keep them frozen! The bears cannot be trusted. Place them in a chilled cylinder.

Mix the carbon-bearing base substrate with the dark syrup.

Damn the Professor's theory about the milk proteins! Add for disturbing results.

Take the additional gelatinous subjects. These must be submerged fresh. Perfectly safe, vivisected as they are.

Serve and drink down your helpless victims.

This reminds me of something I've seen — I think in a dream. They weren't candy bears, though. The frozen ones. Waiting.

GIN AND MISKATONIC

 Serves 1 (but . . . which one . . . ?)

Medicinals

3 ounces Hendrick's Gin

3 lime wedges

4 to 5 ounces Fever Tree tonic water

1 ounce Hpnotiq liqueur

1 rosemary sprig, trimmed properly OR a Yellow Sign made of lemon rind

Apothecary's Craft

Having selected a highball glass able to accommodate the dose, fill with ice, and add the measure of Dr. Hendrick's fortifier.

Squeeze in fresh lime from three wedges (the number is important—admittedly, we don't know why).

Add the tonic generously; stir to combine.

Pour the Hpnotiq liqueur over the back of a spoon to layer on top and make the subject amenable to the rest of the elixir.

The next bit is important, and your choice will determine much!

Place the cut rosemary sprig prominently in front of the glass. Hendrick insists this is the only way and anything else is too dangerous. He is too cautions. Tonight I shall try thte xanthous triskelion and note what effect it has . . .

Serve by the light of a black lamp to behold an eldritch radiance not meant for the human eye. Look you not upon it directly, nor let the eye linger!

Grassie Hall
Miskatonic U.
I had the very fortunate experience of attending a lecture by Prof. W. Dyer here. It was my first visit to the university and his final lecture.

Lemon rinds to replace the lime wedges.

Yellow or Elder — your choice.

Oh! This is much better!
Hendrick seems to have been wrong!

In effigia veritas

Helsingin yliopisto
Prof. Eërikäinen.

———— So many versions
of the same sign. Despite
what dear O. Baer and
Ms. Die say, I doubt
very much that any one
of them has any protective
effects. I do think we
are meant to think
that they do.

←A
curiously
similar
anting-anting,
P.I.

A popular
version amongst
Misk. scholars

Ashmore Journal

So many textures — they spiral down

Such power—
I can't see through it,
yet it clarifies the vision.
Such vision!

NOG-SOTHOTH: THE LIQUOR AT THE PUNCH BOWL

 Serves as the Gate and the Key for 7 mortal beings of fortitude

Spell Components

4 egg yolks + 4 egg whites separated

⅓ cup + 1 tablespoon sugar

1 pint whole milk

1 cup heavy cream

1 teaspoon freshly grated nutmeg

4 to 8 ounces The Kraken Black Spiced Rum
(depending on how much family is visiting)

1 cup black bubble tea boba tapioca pearls

½ cup light Karo or sugar syrup

Ritual of Manifestation

Froth the yolks in a large bowl with a suitable turbulence inducer and unhurriedly add ⅓ cup sugar, mix until completely dissolved. Set this abomination aside.

In a 'saucepan,' swirl together a vortex of milk, cream, and the nutmeg—stir as it begins to bubble. Now remove it from heat and combine with the yolk mixture previously set aside. Bring this new admixture to 160 degrees F, then remove it from the heat. Let stir the Kraken at this point, stir in, and allow to chill for one hour.

Heed well these instructions, for the next steps create unnatural states! Beat the white remainder of the four eggs to soft peaks with the turbulence inducer. With the device still oscillating, add the tablespoon of sugar. Will stiff peaks to form.

Whisk now the egg whites into the mixture, and—if you of strong spirit would complete the ritual in full and shatter all previous conceptions of nog—spoon into your goblet the pearls prepared as described below!

Adding Sothoth to Your Nog— Preparing the Black Bubble Tea Boba Tapioca Pearls

Boil the pearls in water until they break the surface and float. Stir them that they may not adhere. Reduce the heat slightly and cook uncovered for 10 agonizing minutes, stirring occasionally. Remove the saucepan from the heat and let stand for 15 minutes. Drain and rinse the pearls, contain them in a small receptacle, and submerge them in the syrup of Karo before adding to the nog.

HERBERT WEST'S DEANIMATOR

This version has all the desired effects! The fresher the subject, the more apparent the efficacy. Warning: Polluted subjects deanimate very quickly at this potency!

 Makes 1 fast-acting dose (per 150 pounds subject body weight)

Reagent Components

2 ounces Santoni's Limoncello

½ ounce of the spirit of St-Germain

1 dash blue curactao

2 ounces VDKA 6100 solution

Reagent Synthesis

Bind together the Santoni's formula and the St-Germain in an Erlenmeyer flask.

Add the slightest dash of the cerulean stabilizer: less than a quarter ounce, or you'll ruin the effect. It is critical; excess leads to overcompensating with the other ingredients . . . which can have dire consequences.

Lastly, dilute with the VDKA 6100 solution.

You may decant doses from the flask, but a large syringe used to administer orally is . . . better.

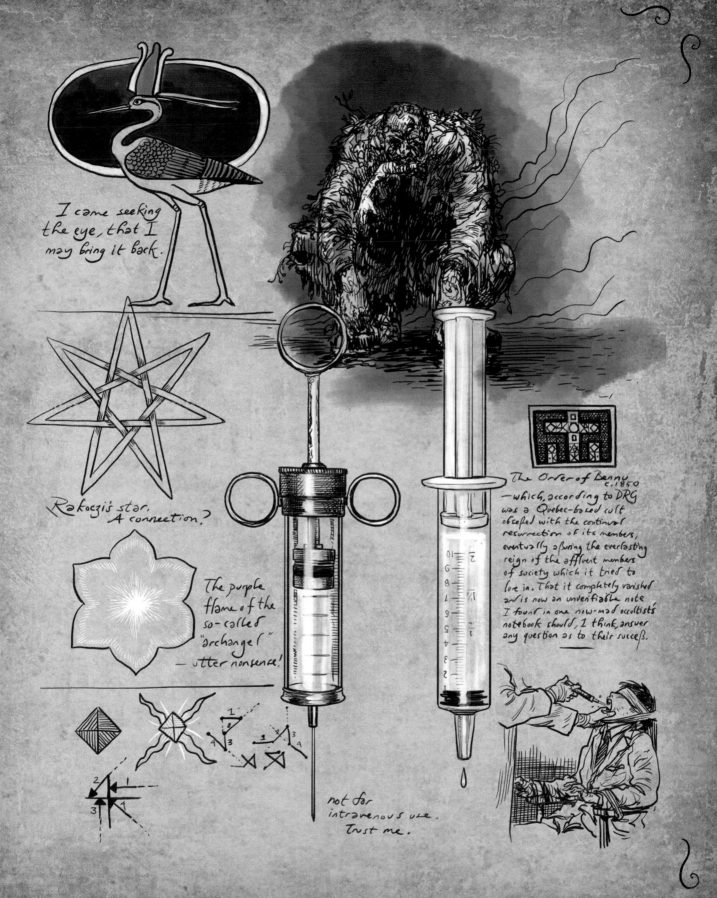

I came seeking the eye, that I may bring it back.

Rakoczi's star. A connection?

The purple flame of the so-called "archangel" — utter nonsense!

not for intravenous use. Trust me.

The Order of Benny c. 1850 — which, according to DRG was a Quebec-based cult obsessed with the continual resurrection of its members, eventually assuring the everlasting reign of the affluent members of society which it tried to lure in. That it completely vanished and is now an unverifiable note I found in one now-mad occultist's notebook should, I think, answer any question as to their success.

MI-GO BRAIN CYLINDER

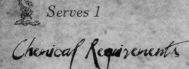 *Serves 1*

Chemical Requirements

1 ounce ScHNaP$_2$S compound, Scottish variant, buttered subtype

1 tablespoon chilled Celtic spirit (creamed)

1 drop Red Ice, isotope 101

Procedure

Utilizing a target-commodious ferromagnetic cylinder, fill to half capacity with the ScHNaP$_2$S compound base.

Pour the creamed celtic syrum over the reverse of a concave metallic transfer implement, a spoon perhaps, to add without haste.

Finally, initiate gravity-assisted insertion of the isotopic solution with a dropper of eyes, force one drop of the Red Ice into the center of the liquid mass.

Subject to cryo-storage if not administering immediately.

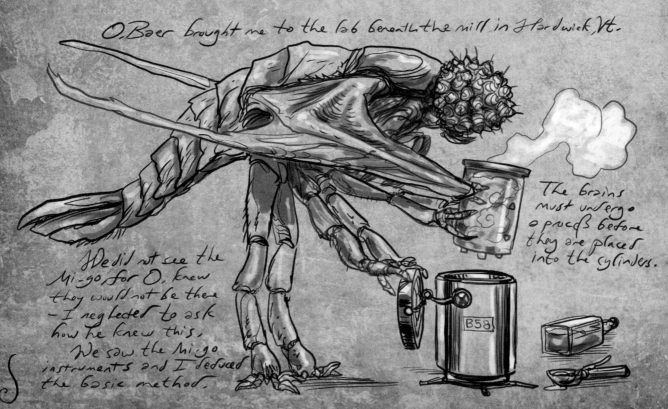

O. Baer brought me to the lab beneath the mill in Hardwick, Vt.

We did not see the Mi-go for O. knew they would not be there — I neglected to ask how he knew this. We saw the Mi-go instruments and I deduced the basic method.

The brains must undergo a process before they are placed into the cylinders.

APPETIZERS

The three components must be pierced together and consumed as one.

Old, old memories here. Not mine (are they?)

Can't shake the greasy feeling, like it coats my thoughts

28

SUNKEN MOO

Serves 4 degenerate primates

Harvested Nutriments

1 cup fresh parsley

1 teaspoon dried oregano

3 tablespoons fresh lemon juice

2 large cloves of garlic, 1 whole,
    1 minced savagely

¼ cup + 5 tablespoons
    extra virgin olive oil

¼ cup water

1½ pounds sirloin steak,
    ruthlessly cubed into 1-inch pieces

30 cherry tomatoes

1 teaspoon salt

1 teaspoon sundered black pepper

2 cups kale, rent into raw shreds

Need for Labors

Conserve your strength. Use a blending artifice to combine the parsley, oregano, and lemon juice with the whole clove, ¼ cup of the olive oil, and the water. Consider just bending one of the monkey spawn to the task. Stop when the liquid is green in hue. Seal a majority of this in an amorphous container with the cubed cattle meat. Allow the ichor to penetrate the cubes, imbuing them with its essence, then place the cubes in the cold for half an hour. Save the unused residue to submerge the final elements.

Coat the tomatoes with 2 tablespoons of the oil, and thence with also the salt and pepper. Put these on a heat transfer foil upon a metal slab, and place into a 375 degree F oven, as we did with the recalcitrant ones in the lost days. Unlike those times, remove them before they burn and as they start to burst.

Oil and heat a small skillet to medium-high, add the kale and remaining garlic, sauté until wilted, dark, and utterly defeated. Season with salt and pepper.

Cook the marinated cattle meat in a larger skillet with the remaining olive oil over medium-high heat, turning frequently, to desired rarity. Skewer all elements, drape with the green remains, and devour.

THE GRAPE OLD WONS

 Serves 4 Who Would Serve (4 appetizers per person)

The Sacrifice

The skins of 16 of the wanton and willing

¼ pound uncased sausage from the Mediterranean

¼ pound slaughtered and pulversized cattle

16 ounces shredded from the neophytes Colby, Monterey, and Jack

½ cup of the White Ichor of Hellmann

¼ cup soured cream

¼ cup whole milk

2 tablespoons mixture from the Ranch hidden in the Valley

16 large firm black or red grapes, peeled and hallowed

1 ounce Emerald Powder of Wa sab-i

Season of Srira'cha

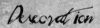

Desecration

In the time before the meat of the slain and flame combine, press the skin wrappings into the receptacles of a muffin slab with wan-ton abandon. Be sure to shape the skins in the manner pleasing to those who shall inhabit them (eyelids or petals).

Imbue the preheated chamber with the strength of 350th degree F and cook for 3 minutes, such that the skin is still pliable. Set aside.

Combine the two fleshes over medium heat until the hue of life has fled, and is drained away. The Sacred Seven, in minutes, should suffice. In an amply sized bowl, fuse this flesh then with the other various tinctures and essences—but not the grapes nor wasabi paste nor Sriracha—until uniform.

Implant 2 tablespoons of the mixture into each skin wrapping form, and return to heat following the same ritual requirements as before for 7 to 8 minutes or until heated through.

Force the wasabi powder evenly onto the eviscerated fruit, dotting each one in the center. Press each grape, so prepared, into the flesh vessels to summon forth the eyes. Spatter with red humor of Sriracha, enfold the eyes within their lids.

Serve faithfully, serve warm! Arise the Grape Old Wons! Iä! Iä!!

Sentinel Hill

p. 751

Who is Whitford?

whispers of the Tocantue

Cross's tells me that bees communicate with each other by dancing. What sentence is this?

Memories of the scarlet dancers of Leng.

Curse of the whippoorwills on Lammas Night, 1929

Sacrifices shall be acquired under darkness and with all due haste and silence lest ye serve next

Hexagonal stepping patterns of the Leng dancers. Why am I just seeing this now?

Embellishment of the cult seal as found scrawled on the wall of the High Tower church by DRG.

The pattern of the honeycomb keeps reoccurring in my life. Can't stop thinking about it.

SACRIFICIAL LAMB

Serves the Black Goat of the Woods!
(or 4 of her faithful)

What Must Be Given

1½ pounds lamb, flayed and slabbed

1 cup each parsley, cilantro, and mint, roughly chopped

1 teaspoon ground ginger (soulless)

2 garlic cloves, crushed mercilessly

1 teaspoon paprika

½ teaspoon ground cinnamon

Essential salts and the common black pepper, cracked

Honey, for brushing and dipping

2 gnarled fistfuls bean sprouts

What Must Be Done

In a crystalline vessel, place the prepared animal sacrifice and layer atop all other sacraments, excepting the salt, the black spice, sweet honey nectar, and the bean sprouts.

Begin the chant, and maintain it as you or a minion combine all the contents of the vessel thoroughly. Set aside and allow half of one hour to recover your mana while it marinates.

Thread now the sacrifice onto metal or wooden stakes, and season with the purifying salt and the black spice.

On a grill or griddle with high heat, cleanse with flame the impaled sacrifice. Achieve an even brown on one side, then apply flame to the other side for an additional minute. Brush with sweet nectar and sear before laying upon a bed of sprouts.

Provide those who will come for the offering a small bowl of the nectar for dipping. Iä! Iä! Shub-Niggurath! The Goat with a Thousand Yum!

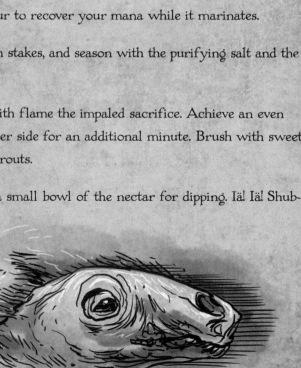

ATLACH-NACHOS

 Serves (the) 8 (Legged Queen of the Chasm to Dream)

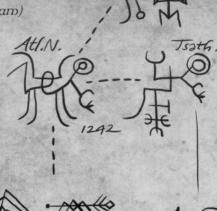

Ingredients

½ pound shredded brisket or pulled pork or chicken

Taco seasoning, to taste

10 to 12 ounces each salsa, guacamole, and sour cream

36 tortilla cups and flat round tortilla chips

20 slices thinly sliced mild Cheddar slices

1 (8-ounce) bag shredded fiesta cheese mix

40 black olives, sliced

30 jalapeños, sliced thinly

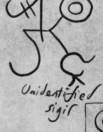

Preparation

Stoke the fire of the oven to the 350th degree F. Anoint the cooked flesh shreds with the powders of the southern tribes. Separate this mixture into thirty-six offerings, and set aside.

Combine the salsa, guacamole, and sour cream to make the viscera, one part each of green, white, and red, mix incompletely, by your own hand.

Lay the thrice dozen outer carapace tortilla shells on a large tray. Spoon into each a pleasing measure of visceral paste. Halve each meat offering, and cross the halves to make an X in each shell, then cover with a slice of Cheddar slightly larger than the cup itself. Bake until the cheese melts and the seal is complete.

Allow to cool, then flip each cup over.

Scatter the fiesta cheese filaments generously on the top of each. Upon these, place two olive rings in front, and a slice of the pepper on the tortilla "back," on top of the cheese. Bake, as under the merciless sun of unknown skies, for 2 more minutes. The horde then stands ready to consume.

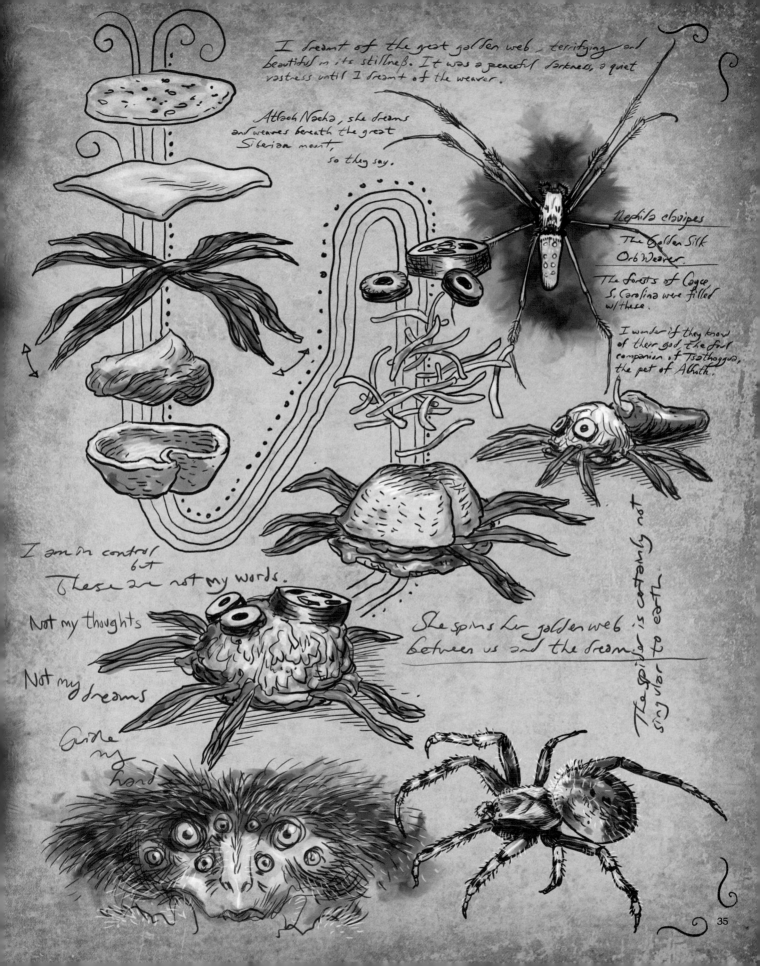

I dreamt of the great golden web, terrifying and beautiful in its stillness. It was a peaceful darkness, a quiet vastness until I dreamt of the weaver.

Atlach Nacha, she dreams and weaves beneath the great Siberian mount, so they say.

Nephila clavipes
The Golden Silk Orb Weaver.

The forests of Cayce S. Carolina were filled w/ these.

I wonder if they know of their god, the first companion of Tsathoggua, the pet of Atlach.

I am in control but

These are not my words.

Not my thoughts

Not my dreams

Guide my hand

She spins her golden web between us and the dream.

The spider is certainly not singular to earth.

35

SOUPS AND SALADS

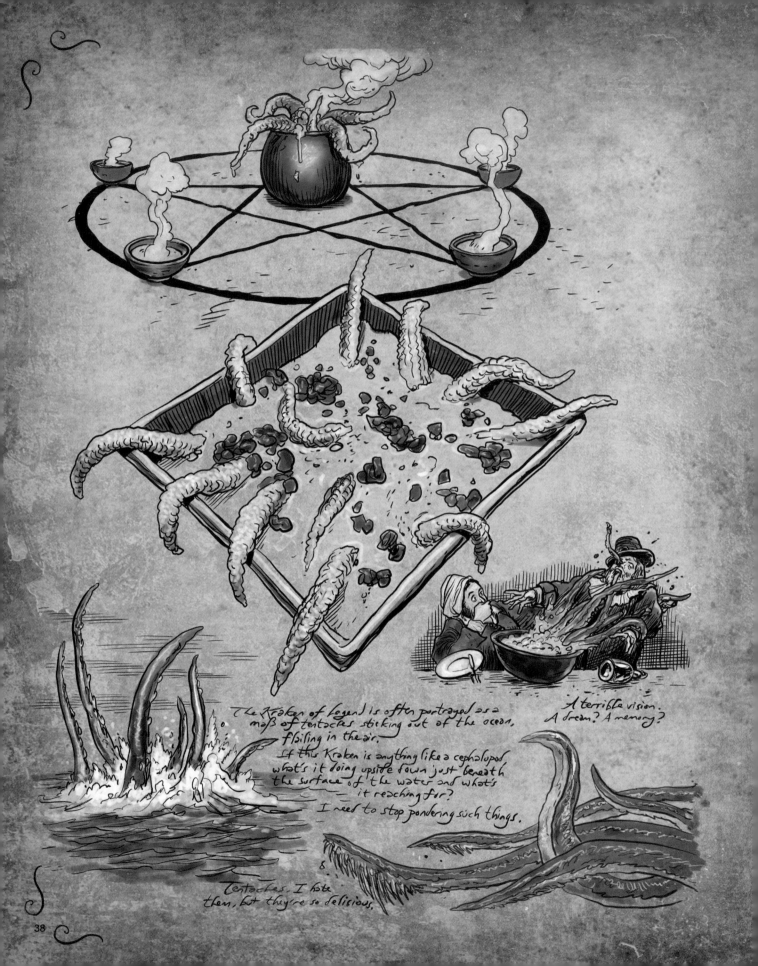

The Kraken of Legend is often portrayed as a mass of tentacles sticking out of the ocean, flailing in the air.

If this Kraken is anything like a cephalopod what's it doing upside down just beneath the surface of the water and what's it reaching for?

I need to stop pondering such things.

A terrible vision. A dream? A memory?

Tentacles. I hate them, but they're so delicious.

NEW ENGLAND DAMNED CHOWDER

 Serves 5, as each of the corners in an inverted pentagram

Sacrifices

5 center-cut bacon strips, thick cut

1 small onion, finely diced

2 stalks celery, chopped

2 small cloves garlic, sliced or mashed

4 potatoes, cubed

1 cup water

1 (8-ounce) bottle clam juice

4 teaspoons chicken bouillon

½ teaspoon white pepper

½ teaspoon thyme

¼ cup all-purpose flour

2½ cups heavy cream, divided equally

2 (51-ounce) cans chopped clams

1 bunch scallions, diced, for garnish

Blasphemous Rite

In a dutch oven or other capacious cooking vessel, cook the swine meat of divine glory over medium heat. One quarter hours should see them crisp, remove then to parchment to drain. Squander not the juices of the meat, for now shalt thou baptise the onion, celery, and garlic, sautéing one twelfth hour or until tender. As for the fate of the potatoes: add them now, along with the water, clam juice, boullion, pepper, and thyme.

Boil it! Boil it all! Once at a boil, reduce heat.

Patience now, Brothers and Sisters . . . simmer unveiled for 15 to 20 minutes or until the many cubed are tender.

In a small skull bowl, combine the flour and 1½ cups of the heavy cream until smooth. Stir this slowly into the rest. Bring all to a boil; mutter the incantation, as instructed below, and stir until thickened.

Complete now your clamnation! Add slowly the clams as well as the remaining heavy cream, and put it again to the flame until warmed through, yet not boiling. Crumble in the reserved bacon, Prince of Meats, leaving some for a garnish on top.

Garnish with sprinkles of the scallions and echoing laughter.

Incantation

"Apud gratia canatantes ana marie apud latias malus."

wetting
the hands to
mold the rice.

PALLID BISQUE

 Serves 4 to 6, once-and then, madness

Dramatis Personae

3 tablespoons unsalted butter

2 tablespoons chopped green onion

2 tablespoons chopped celery

2½ cups milk

3 tablespoons all-purpose flour

½ teaspoon freshly ground black pepper

1 tablespoon paste of the tomato

1 cup heavy cream of whipping

8 ounces meat from the Clawed Scuttler

4 to 8 ounces cooked, shelled Craw Fathers or other minor seabeasts

4 tablespoons sherry

¼ teaspoon salt

1 cup sticky rice

4 to 6 dollops of soured cream (1 per serving)

Acts

Camilla melts the butter in a large saucepan over medium-low heat; she adds the chopped green onion and celery. With a forlorn sigh, she sautés and stirs until tender, like her Uoht's gentle hands. She retires, leaving the hovering priest Noatalba to continue the work.

Cassilda warms the milk in another pan over medium heat—a warmth she can never feel for herself.

Noatalba stirs, and with restless hands combines the flour into the butter and garden's yield. For 2 to 3 minutes he goes on, slowly adding the warmed milk. The priest's heavy lids watch roux-fully as the thickening portends—for then he will know to add the black pepper, scarlet paste, and heavy cream.

CHILD: *May I put in the creatures? There are so many. The red-clawed, the small-clawed. The round ones. I do so love them all.*

CASSILDA: [With a hiss] *Yes, but be quick about it!*

[Simmering, she parts reluctantly with her sherry, adding it almost disdainfully to the broth. Noatalba fearfully scatters a pinch of salt, but it is too late. Resigned, he portions the bisque into bowls.]

[All turn toward a dread presence.]

STRANGER: *A rice mask, formed by his own hand—he lays one atop the bisque in each of their bowls. A dollop of sour holds each in place. Curls of water beast flesh form a tri-branched sign.*

ALL: *Mercy!*

THE KING: *Did you think to be hungry still?*

INVESTIGATOR GUMBO

 Feeds the curiosity of 8 intrepid souls

Evidence

1 cup vegetable oil —*for greasing palms?*

1 cup all-purpose flour —*but . . . what purpose?*

1 cup each chopped onion, green and red bell pepper, and chopped celery —*someone did a chop job on all these too*

3 tablespoons minced garlic —*not words, apparently—This happened fast*

3 cups chopped okra —*West African? Ethiopia? Might tell us something . . .*

1½ cups amber or lager beer —*shame what they did to that beer*

6 cups seafood or chicken stock —*one for the lab boys, I can't tell which it is.*

2 bay leaves —*Why two? Why any . . . ? They must be significant.*

2 teaspoons Cajun or "Old Bay" seasoning —*Spilled carefully? Struggle?*

1 tablespoon apple cider vinegar —*I hear that's good for a lot. Like removing fingerprints.*

2 tablespoons kosher salt —*The salt is all that's kosher about this scene . . .*

1½ teaspoons cayenne pepper —*Crushed without teeth. What has that kind of strength?*

1 pound medium fresh shrimp or crawfish —*Cripes! Looks like their veins have been ripped from them, heads removed, and peeled right out of their shells. Hell of a way to go.*

1 pound red snapper fillets or white fish —*chopped so badly—I can't be sure which.*

2 cups shucked oysters —*someone played a shell game with them—they lost.*

1 cup crab meat —*looks like it took its lumps before someone picked it clean*

½ pound alligator meat —*I don't see evidence of cutting—this looks torn! What could . . . ?*

¼ cup chopped parsley —*fresh—it hasn't been long. Maybe they're still here?*

2 tablespoons filé powder —*I have some questions for this "Zatarian" when we catch up with him*

Hot cooked rice for 8 —*It's like they knew . . .*

Green onion, roughly chopped, for garnish —*if desired?*

The Cthulian is a be—

The Scene

In an 8-quart stockpot is where it all ended up. First, they heated the oil over medium heat for about 5 minutes, by the looks of it; then, in went the flour. This would have formed a roux . . . the color of peanut butter, in about 15 to 20 minutes.

Next, the onion, bell peppers, celery, garlic, and okra got it—right in—no finesse. State they were in, they never felt a thing. After a few minutes, maybe 5, they added the beer, stock, bay leaves, Cajun seasoning, vinegar, salt, and cayenne. Brings me to a boil thinking about it—but I don't get to reduce the heat, and it simmers for the next hour.

Last in was the shrimp, fish, oysters, crab meat, and the gator. It was over once you added gator to the mix. Might have taken 8, 10 minutes until they were cooked through. The parsley was an afterthought. Always is.

Filé this one under "powder" just before serving. It's all thoroughly mixed up. Rice working with you. This one was a real mess. Hope they don't garnish my green—there'd be tears.

the combination
of shapes:
maddening.

When I look into
it, I feel watched!

Perhaps a lone wedge is safer
until I know more.

Be careful with
the arrangement.
When dealing with
such things,
just the right
geometry can be
cataclysmic!

44

DINING TRAPEZOHEDRON

 Serves Nyarlathotep, and 4 Starry Wisdom acolytes

Four-Dimensional Manifestations

2 small tomatoes, diced
(any decahedral configuration will do)

Kosher salt to taste

4 to 6 slices of bacon

½ cup bread crumbs

Freshly ground black pepper

4 tablespoons brown sugar

1 titanic head of a glacier cabbage, drained of all
vitality *(in modern texts, "iceberg
lettuce")*

1 small red onion, minced viciously

Dressing

*(Shortcuts may be taken here, but they
have a price. Your merchant will know
what is needed.)*

2 ounces sharp blue cheese

½ cup viscous white doom *(I can guide you
through the Maze of N'Ich...)*

½ cup soured cream

½ cup unwholesome milk

1 tablespoon juice of citrus in yellow

Freshly ground black pepper to taste

To See Bey and Mortal Ken

Set a mesh of metal over a small bowl and add diced tomatoes—if they appear unruly, it is only the light. Sprinkle with the blessed salt and toss evenly (oddly if the moon shows through the trees). Set aside.

In a small skillet, cook the salted flesh of the swine over medium-high heat, until crisped. This offering must not be burnt! Transfer to a parchment-laden plate. *(You know the one)*

Using some of the rendered fat, add bread crumbs and cook over medium heat until browned and crisp. Transfer to a new parchmented plate to drain, and anoint with the spices of light and darkness.

Take up the blade, rend the meat into fine bits. Turn the flame low, cook again the cooked chopped bacon until crisped and deep

brown. Thus prepared, set the remains upon parchment. Clean your skillet, and reheat on medium-low. Add the bacon and brown sugar, stirring, stirring. . . . A transmogrification will begin; watch it closely that it does not burn. *I approach. Absolution!* Once cloaked in the glaze thus evoked, remove from heat; cool.

Preparing the Raiment: In a medium vessel, whisk away those milky things unmentionable, the juice of the lemon; add the black spice when congealed.

Blaze the lights! *It will avail you not.*

Bring forth the lettuce head, shorn of its outer layers and quartered through the core so that each quarter holds together. Arrange these wedges on plates and dole the pale dressing upon each. Bestow on these the red onion at a strange angle. Add all else, for it is done.

Wait for me.

MAIN DISHES

The Order of Tsathoggua

TSATHOGGUAMBALAJA

 Serves 4 to 6 who remember the red-lit caverns and the One Who Dwells There

What Must Be Offered

3 tablespoons olive oil

½ medium onion, chopped

½ green bell pepper, chopped

1 celery stalk, chopped

½ pound andouille sausage, sliced into thin disks

3 cups cooked rice

1 teaspoon each paprika, black pepper, and dried oregano

½ teaspoon each onion powder and dried thyme

¼ teaspoon garlic salt

1 bay leaf

2 cups chicken broth

1 cup water

1 tablespoon tomato paste

½ teaspoon hot pepper sauce—or more, half measures are for the weak of faith!

28 ounces canned diced tomatoes, undrained

½ pound shrimp, split, cleansed, and without shell

¼ pound tuna or any unwary finned sea denizen, rend this offering to chunks

¼ pound clams, mussels, or scallops—see that these are cooked

2 tablespoons chopped fresh parsley

The Rite

The Eve of May and the Eve of All Hallows are best, but good result may be had at other times if Cykranosh is visible.

Using the Dutch method over a medium-high heat, bathe the onion, bell pepper, celery, and sausage in the sacred oil of the olive for 5 to 10 blessed minutes. When they are tender, add the rice and all the spices, including the leaf of bay. Cook these together for a space of 2 minutes.

Add then the broth, water, tomato paste, pepper sauce, and the undrained tomatoes. Boil this, then cover from the eyes of the followers of the hated upstart. Reduce heat, let all simmer until the hour approaches one-third. Then add the beasts from the sea, ritual effigy of the foe. Continuing to simmer, let vengeance seethe, let vengeance stand, for 5 minutes. Now, at half the hour, remove the leaf. It has served its purpose. Stir in the parsley. It is done.

AHIÄ! AHIÄ! FATHER DAGON!

 Serves 4 with the Look

Ritual Offerings

3¾ pounds tuna steak—it must be taken fresh

1¼ cups oil of the Middle Lander's olives —they will tithe willingly

5 limes, zest grated and squeezed of vitae to create 1 cup

2½ tablespoons sauce from the Far East, salty and dark as the Sea itself

2 tablespoons flame of Tabas Koh, if it pleases you

2½ tablespoons blessed salt

1½ tablespoons freshly milled black pepper

1 cup chopped scallions, the white and the green
   —Sea and Shore, finely mingled

3¼ tablespoons of the Aztec's favored fruit, minced
   —without seed, if the warmth pleases

5 ripe avocados—Old Man Hass can get them safely from the savage kin

1½ tablespoons seeds of sesame, touched of fire

Four fresh rings of the apple of pine

The Conjugation

A large stoneware vessel shall contain the fresh-caught offering, cubed, as the sunken blocks of lost Y'ha-nthlei, but to the fourth of the inch.

In the second vessel you shall commingle the oil from the middle lands, skin and fluids of the lime, the Sauce of S'oy, the juice that burns, the blessed salt, and the black spice. Use this to anoint the offered flesh, adding the greens of the shore and the Aztec fruit, and mixing with lusty abandon under moonlight.

Seize the avocados. Cleave the gifts of the swamp brethren in twain. Remove their hard hearts, and peel off their flesh. These also make into the likeness of the blocks our forefathers carved for our mighty cities. Once cubed, they are added to the rest, so shall we rebuild what was lost—the seeds are replanted! As Below, Within.

Set in the Artifice of Winter for one twelfth of the daylight hours to allow for proper impregnation. Then, with the palm and the web of the hand, form 2½-inch spheres, and serve on a bed of rice or quinoa, topped with the golden rings.

The Sea! The Grain! Father Dagon! Iä! Iä!

Give a man a fish, he eats for a day.
Make a man a fish...

SOUTH

Devil's Reef

D. Mauer

1978

— "D. Mauer?" David Maurer?
Found by the mill, near the creek.

Fair Winds and Following Seas,
old friend.

He had the look

- pineapple -
- lime -
- tortilla chip -

The avocado and tuna
can be prepared separately and
stacked as a cylinder, but this
requires greater skill and incurs
a greater risk!

A
T

A
T

51

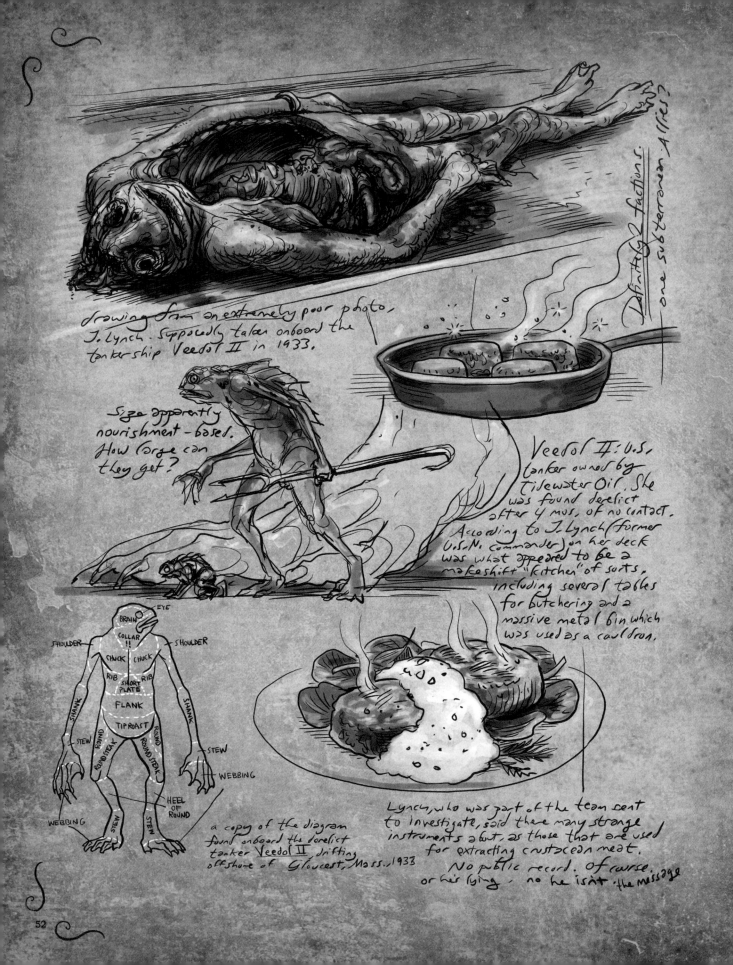

drawing from an extremely poor photo, J. Lynch. supposedly taken onboard the tanker ship Veedol II in 1933.

Definitely factions. one subterranean. Allies?

Size apparently nourishment-based. How large can they get?

Veedol II: U.S. tanker owned by Tidewater Oil. She was found derelict after 4 mos. of no contact. According to J. Lynch (former U.S.N. commander) on her deck was what appeared to be a makeshift "kitchen" of sorts, including several tables for butchering and a massive metal bin which was used as a cauldron.

BRAIN
EYE
COLLAR !!
SHOULDER
SHOULDER
CHUCK CHUCK
RIB RIB
SHORT PLATE
FLANK
SHANK
SHANK
TIP ROAST
ROUND
ROUND
STEW
ROUND STEAK
ROUND STEAK
STEW
WEBBING
HEEL OF ROUND
WEBBING
STEW
STEW

a copy of the diagram found onboard the derelict tanker Veedol II drifting offshore of Gloucest. Mass. 1933

Lynch, who was part of the team sent to investigate, said there many strange instruments about. as those that are used for extracting crustacean meat.
No public record. Of course. or he's lying. no he isn't .the message

52

DEEP-FRIED DEEP ONE

Serves 4 of them right

Offerings to Vengeance

1 large egg of the fowl of the wood, as Sadogui doth favor

1 tablespoon of the best offering to be found in the Maze of N'yo

—use the Eye of Azoth, it is too dangerous to go in body. The Hunter will abide this small trespass. We know.

1 teaspoon seasoning from the Old Bay of Elders

¼ teaspoon salt of the Sea

1 teaspoon finely chopped Herb of Mysterious Purpose

1 pound lump crabmeat, ritually cleansed and purified

½ pound fresh pink-fleshed fish of the river and sea

1½ tablespoons unseasoned crumbs of bread, more if needed

3 tablespoons unsalted butter, to ease the transition

Wedges of the Citrus in Yellow are always welcome . . .

Visitation of Wrath

Make ready an altar of flat metal, line this with the alchemical foil.

In a commodious vessel, join forcibly the egg, mayonnaise, the spice of the Bay of Elders, salt, and parsley. Take the flesh of the sea dwellers, mingle them blasphemously in the eyes of their Sleeping Lord. Fold all this now together, with care that flesh can still be recognized. When this is done, raise the bowl high, twice, then sprinkle with the crumbs. Lower the bowl to the Earth that the One Below may see what has been done in His name!

Shape, in the old way, into eight disks, and place upon the prepared altar. Cast them into the darkness and cold for one twelfth of one of your numbered days.

Heat the salve of transition in the proper implement and exult as the disks sizzle and brown! Brown them as the sun would the husks of our briny foe, turning them and cooking each side for 4 minutes. They are delicate—have care if you wish the centre to hold!

Remember the Mongol and the Turk when they came to aid us in Averoigne. We remember our allies, and we shall serve together again!

THE FISHES FROM OUTSIDE

Serves 4 Who Dare

Incantation

Two large snapper fish, gutted clean

Twelve and three large garlic cloves

minced and combined with salt of coves

Two teaspoons ground cumin gleaned

Two teaspoons ground coriander

One teaspoon black pepper from rack

One teaspoon also ground sumac

One half cup chopped fresh dill to stir

Four bell peppers, different hues

Two large tomatoes, onions red

Sliced to rounds and, plated and spread

Olive oil and two lemons choose

The Summoning

Preheat oven four twenty-five
Pat the snapper until well dry
With a sacred knife, make slits lie
Upon the flesh, upon each side
Fill the slits, coat gut cavity
Of each fish with the garlic chopped
Mix spices with which they'll be topped
Most of this pat round thoroughly
Keep the rest for its later use
Stuff each fish with the chopped dill
And much sliced veggies as you will
On an oiled sheet all introduce
Add of the veggies what remains
To form a frame around the fish
Sprinkle rest of mix, if you wish
Drizzle oil like Zimbabwe's rains
Place sheet upon the lower rack
Of oven heated as foretold
Twenty-five min 'til flakes unfold
Move to a platter now to hack
In lemon juice shall cover all
Using slits rend both fish in twain
Portion morsels like fisher crane
Serve with wedges, before They call

Mourner again
— what were you
up to?

Symmetry in the stocking
is key but the lines of
the scale are otherworldly

55

"Yoth—it lay below K'n-yan
the red light...does nothing
to banish the darkness that
moves!"
— Final entry
journal of D. Visalle
— found near Alabaster Caverns,
Moorland, OK -- Suggests she
made it back, but where is she?

Arrange your spawn effigies upon
the plate in a most unattractive manner.

FORMLESS SPAWNGHETTI

 Creates 12 Spawn

To Summon the Spawn

½ pound squid ink pasta

4 tablespoons lemon juice

2 tablespoons olive oil

A generous pinch of lemon zest

2 chopped cloves garlic

2 tablespoons capers

2 cups chicken broth

1 teaspoon rosemary salt

½ teaspoon oregano

½ teaspoon parsley

5 tablespoons unsalted butter

1 pound of small, cooked shrimp, stripped of their shell and vein

3 (10.5-ounce) packages breadstick dough

1 cup halved cherry tomatoes

The Invocation

Prepare the black tendrils according to tradition. Drain, rinse, and remove to a vessel capable of holding them. Mindful of errant seeds, crush the yellow fruit in thy fist, that its vitae and pulped flesh rain onto the mass of tendrils.

With great heat and oil combine the zest, garlic, and caper madly. Then add the fowl broth, essential salt, oregano, and parsley, then the butter to boil. Simmer this until it thickens of its own accord. Place the Curled Ones in the preparation, coating them well, and turning them as they simmer.

During the Time of Simmering, bring forth the formless breadstick mass from its prison. Conform it by force into the Twelve Wells of Pan.

When this is done, lay in each well a mass of the black tendrils, let them spill forth chaotically. Upon them, heap the anointed shrimp and their residue generously. Pinch closed the wells, leaving tendrils spilling forth from the top or any apertures that present.

For one-sixth hour, subject them to the preheated 375th degree F in a red-litten kiln until tones of golden brown appear on the exterior, the tendrils stiffen and crisp. Garnish with the split red fruits, then serve under the new moon.

TO CALL FORTH THE SANDWICH HORROR

What Ye Must Gather

1 round pretzel bread roll (with four-pointed-star pattern, or else all is lost)

1 whole olive, stuffed with cheese of goat

1 pound rare roast beef, deli-sliced thin

3 to 5 pickle spears, skinned

1 roasted red pepper

1 cup almond shards

A disc of Swiss cheese, sliced thin, torn roughly round

Green pesto sauce

The Rite

Using a ceremonial blade prepared with the proper incantations, remove the centre of star from the top of the bun; ignore any protest from the bun. This shall serve as the socket for the eye. Now insert an olive, which has been ritually eviscerated and stuffed with the cheese of a black goat.

With the eye thusly in place, set aside this portion of the creature, and pile the lower bun half with the bloody meat of the cow. Position the last inch or so of your pickle spears as you like. Nestle them firmly into the heaped bloody remains of the cow so that most of these tentacles protrude onto the plate.

On top of this, place the whole roasted pepper, with the open end facing the "front." Insert into this opening the almond shards. This shall be the mouth and teeth.

Rend the cheese artfully to remove the corners (always beware the corners!). It should be roughly round. Place this on top of the pepper. You may wish to apply flame to the cheese now to melt it slightly if you have the knowledge and tools to do so.

Now for the last—drizzle the green ichor across the tentacles, Eye of Yog-Sothoth (and anywhere else your sense of the aesthetic demands).

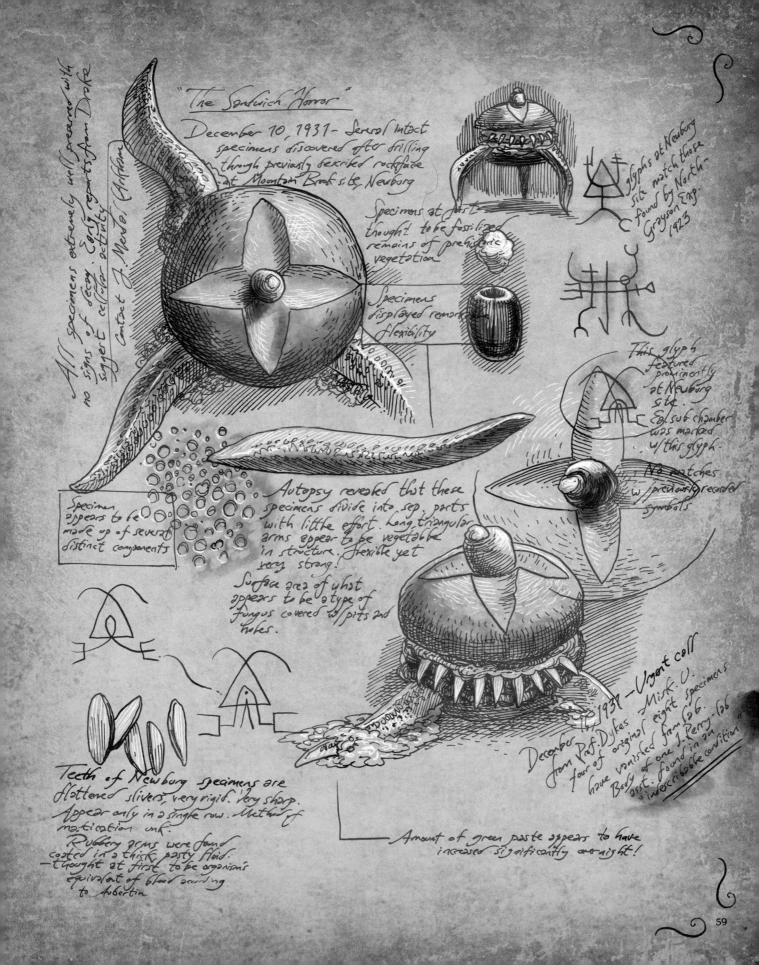

"The Sandwich Horror"

December 10, 1931 - Several intact specimens discovered after drilling through previously detected rockface at Mountain Brook site, Newburg

All specimens extremely well preserved with no signs of decay. Early reports from Drake suggest cellular activity. Contact J. Mendez (Arkham)

Specimens at first thought to be fossilized remains of prehistoric vegetation

Specimens displayed remarkable flexibility

glyphs at Newburg site match those found by North-Grayson Exp. 1923

Specimen appears to be made up of several distinct components

This glyph featured prominently at Newburg site. Ex. sub chamber was marked w/ this glyph. No matches w/ previously recorded symbols

Autopsy revealed that these specimens divide into sep. parts with little effort. Long triangular arms appear to be vegetable in structure. Flexible yet very strong!

Surface area of what appears to be a type of fungus covered w/ pits and holes.

Teeth of Newburg specimens are flattened slivers, very rigid. Very sharp. Appear only in a single row. Method of mastication unk.
- Rubbery arms were found coated in a thick pasty fluid.
- thought at first to be organism's equivalent of blood according to Aubertin

December 11, 1931 - Urgent call from Prof. Dykes - Misk. U. four of original eight specimens have vanished from lab. Body of one J. Perry - lab asst. found in an "indescribable condition"

Amount of green paste appears to have increased significantly overnight!

59

BYAKHEE GYRO

Serves 6 who would ply the void

To Make Ready

1 medium onion, finely chopped, plus more for serving

2 pounds ground lamb

1 tablespoon each finely minced garlic,
   dried marjoram, and dried ground rosemary

2 teaspoons kosher salt

½ teaspoon freshly ground black pepper

1 brick of clay, wrapped moldable metal sheets

6 pieces of pita bread with chopped
   tomato and feta cheese for consumption

16 ounces plain yogurt

1 medium cucumber, peeled, seeded, and finely chopped

Pinch of blessed salt

3 cloves garlic, finely minced

1 tablespoon olive oil

2 teaspoons vinegar from red wine

6 mint leaves, finely minced

To Travel the Void

Five things thou wilt need when Aldebaran doth shine: a whistle, the Elder Sign, the sure Blades of Processor of Food, a purified clay brick of the proper size—enrobed in silvery metal, and a Diviner of Warmth.

Put the onion to The Blades. With a cloth for the purpose, dry the remains—their ordeal is not complete. Again cut them, but in company with the lamb, garlic, marjoram, rosemary, salt, and pepper. Reduce these to a commingled slurry within the cruel, uncaring device.

Prepare your kiln. It should reach the 325th degree of the Heights of Farran. The brick you shall heat as well. Fold the slurry into the loaf pan, being certain that the Void cannot seep in at the edges!

In a larger baking vessel, bathe the pan in water, and bake for 1 hour or until the temperature within the mixture reaches the 165th degrees, according to our Diviner of Warmth. Remove then, and doth cleanse of any fatty congelation.

Place now the brick directly upon the surface of the meat and compress by the bounds of gravity—which you are soon to shed! When the Diviner reveals the 175th degree, it is done. This should take the space of a quarter to a third of an hour. Slice generously and serve on the Bread of Pita, with onion, tomato, and cheese feta.

The secret of the sauce of the Tzatziki is simple: combine the yogurt, cucumber, salt, garlic, oil of the olive, vinegar, and mint!

Tell no one.

Serve with space mead, for a pleasant journey.

They didn't so much fly as they crawl and tumble through the misty air.

She reminded me of some sickly, rotting animal corpse in a swamp.

the Festival Mead . . .

the heat metal-enshrouded brick completes the cooking process

They aren't from here

They're leaving them here.

Constantly tittering, chattering, shuddering

Where is the Stone Key? What does it have to do w/ the mead?

1st from Greece

Necessary nourishment for the journey.

Oh the piping, The ceaseless piping!

— Twist their heads off!

Winooski River, near Montpelier, Vt.
West River in Windham County, past Newfane, Vt.
Passumpsic River in Caledonia County, above Lyndonville, Vt.
— bodies found but no evidence beyond
eyewitness testimony for the bodies fell to
less than dust, for their matter was not
of this world.
Could they have drowned in the
Vermont flood waters? I think not.

— Abashed the devil stood
and felt how awful
goodness was

Death is the
escape from time.

Who why does the voice
keep changing?

Vermont Pink
as Prof. Dykes
calls them, though
he has never
seen one and
they cannot
be photographed.

They lived and operated
deep w/in those Vermont
hills. They are still
here somewhere.

They speak
like a great
distant swarm
in the howling
wind.

Flightless Siberian
Mi-Go "Abominable Snowman"
based on the description in the J. Bellows journal, 1952

MI-GO TO GO

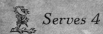 *Serves 4*

Vivisection

4 large portobello-strain fungoides

High purity unrefined oils of the Oleacae species

2 tendril tips each worth of sodium preservative particulate, ebony spice, and allicin-bearing Allium samples

2 large red native fruits—*note these are neither "beef" nor "steak." The taxonomy of the y'cung race remains opaque...*

4 thin circular cross-sections of sharp or smoked Cheddar

4 large cashews, boil or soak these native nut-bodies to soften

4 blackberries

1 sprig thyme

Loose dill

4 ciabatta-strain confection, supplementary

Preparation for Consumption

Lobotomize the fungi by removing their stems. This will make them more pliant to the remainder of the procedure.

Apply lightly the carrier oil on both sides that the flavor augmentation particulates may cling. Adhere the one pinch each of the spices.

Place the seasoned fungi in a shallow high-temperature receptacle, applying light pressure with a paddle limb to ensure the prey does not squirm free during the five minutes it shall cook.

Create thick cross-sections of the robust red native fruit and subject these to the same seasoning procedure followed for the fungi main body. These need not be heated individually, as they possess no sentience to purge. Place these then on top of the fungi and enclose under a dome for 120 seconds.

Now blanket this concoction in the cheese. Replace the dome, and remove from heat. Allow the cultured film to deliquesce, and then remove to feeding platters. Add the nut bodies and berries of black.

Place centrally the main body and heads of larval Fungi upon each portion and engage thyme-dillation protocol to force the wings and limbs to form. From the shallow receptacle, drizzle all with the fluids. Serve openly displayed, on a leavened confection of the ciabatta genus, if you choose.

WILBUR WHATELEY'S DUNWICH SANDWICH

 Serves Those Who Shall Be Eight

Fragments

1 (9-pound) pork shoulder butt roast, with the bone in, flayed

1 bottle Samuel Adams Cream Stout

1 cup apple cider vinegar

1½ bottles Bull's-Eye Original BBQ Ssauce

1 bottle Bull's-Eye Hickory Smoked BBQ Sauce

⅓ cup brown sugar

Garlic powder, onion salt, ground cayenne pepper, and paprika to taste

8 slices Boston Brown Bread

Bread-and-butter pickles

The Open-Faced Way

Grandfather's notes say to place the flesh offering, bathed in the famous brewman's stout and the cider gone to vinegar, in a slow cooker. Then anoint the offering with the original preparation of the Ichor of Bhar-behek qu, sparing the half-part, making certain to engulf the sacrifice completely.

For one half day shall the flame bank low beneath the vessel. When the flesh falls from the bone under the power of Them Who Approach, shall yew know yew have triumphed! Summon forth all o' the bones—they foretell the fate o' Man when opens the Way!

Remove the meat to a wooden slab, and rend it into shreds with great vigor. Remove the bones: all that is not meat must be separated and purged. Drain the liquid from the vessel, saving two-thirds of a cup. The rest is not needed. Put the saved portion into a ceremonial bowl.

Inter the content o' this bowl shall ye coalesce the sweetest darkness, the saltes, fiery spices, the baneroot, an' both the remainder of first, an' all o' the alternate prep'rashun of Bhar-behek'qu's Ichor. When that's be done, put all o' it an' the flesh back into the great vessel.

Upon the warm'd flesh, discharge this elixir an' allow it to be absorb'd by the hungering mass awaitin'. Bank low the flame to maintain its readiness. Ef'n ye want, ye can drain some off ta be held aside fer daubin' what'll burst out when the formula be done.

Apportion for The Eight a generous measure of this—upon the russet slabs. The yellow-emerald eyes of the One Who Waits Between shall adorn and attend directly upon the measures. For this knowledge I have passed. Iä! Sog-Meat'broth! Iä!

I am more perplexed now than when I began my Investigation. It is almost as if the recipes are written by different individuals, but I cannot find any variation in the handwriting. Perhaps they were compiled and transcribed by one person?

Boston Brown Bread
H. Jones Bakery

Upon a bed of Boston Brown Bread, Wilbur Whateley withered and bled.

— Local children's rhyme

Order
of
Dagon

INNSMOUTH SHUCK

 Serves . . . to identify two of the sea blessed

The Sea's Bounty

12 oysters from the Bay of Chesapeake

2 cups of the sailor's might

1 cup arugula

2 onions of spring

3 strips of cooked bacon

1 clove of garlic

1 tablespoon unsalted butter

Fresh lemon to be squeezed for its essence, then abandoned

2 tablespoons hot sauce

¼ cup each grated Gruyère and Parmesan cheeses

The Transformation

Hearken to my tale of woe and salvation. Our instruments were crazed, reading longitude 450 degrees F, and hot as an oven it was that night. The surface of the sea was like wrinkled foil on a sheet of dull metal.

The lads were laid out flat on the deck like lifeless blobs of meat ripped from their shells. We knew something had ta be done, so we threw rationing to the West wind, and my mate an' I determined to take the last of the greens, and even the bacon—chopping them fine to stretch what we had left.

These but the bacon went with the end of th' butter in a small skillet Cyrus had, along with some garlic for health, till all was good an' softened up and the last bit of steam carried our prayers for wind out to the sea.

Licking our lips, we added the bacon then, along with the citrus to keep away a disease that was the least of our worries at the time. A dash of pepper sauce too, and stirred until all moisture fled again.

We took this poultice and spread a bit on each of their bodies, and shook the cheese on 'em for good measure. Oh, how the sun baked them! None of them lasted more than 10 minutes more, despite all our effort.

The sea took their bodies then, we both swear it! Oh, I miss 'em . . . but it was only me and Cyrus what made it back to shore. At night, by the coast, I hear 'em calling, calling still.

SHOGGHOULASH

 Serves 4, under strict hypnotic control

Biological

1⅓ pounds terrestrial cattle meat

Salt and ground black pepper

½ cup diced sweet onion

½ cup green pepper in thin strips

1 clove garlic, minced

14.5-ounce can diced tomatoes, drained

8 ounces red sauce of the Ionian region

3 cups precooked mashed tuberoids, chilled

½ to 1 cup milk

½ cup shredded Cheddar

4 strips bacon, chopped to bits

2 ounces pearl onions

2 ounces cooked black-eyed peas

Powder of Paprii-kah for dusting

Canolic censer of P'aam

Very reminiscent of the luminous eyes of the hopping ghosts!

Creation

Protoplasmic Bulk: In a shallow vessel over strong flame, cook the ground cattle meat with salt and pepper to taste, diced onion, and green pepper until it is light brown. Drain any nonessential fluids and set aside for reasons that will reveal themselves all too quickly. To this, reduce to a moderate flame and introduce the garlic, drained diced tomatoes, and tomato sauce until cooked throughout.

Transfer carefully upon a suitably strong platter.

Primary sense organ implantation: Having previously prepared the potato base, remove it from cryonic storage and combine with quarter to half cup of fluids harvested from terrestrial cattle, Cheddar, crumbled bacon, and sodium.

Form this mass into four spheres, adding quarter to half cup of dairy fluids as needed to achieve cohesion. Implant pearl onions and peas, randomly spaced, into the surface of the spheres. Reform to round shape as necessary.

Preheat the kiln to 425°F. Place the shaped spheres onto a greased metallic sheet. Dust with Powder of Papri-kah and douse with accelerant spray. Bake until golden and warm throughout, approximately one-third hour. Reshape the gibbering mass as necessary. Orient the complete spheroids centrally in the prepared animal bulk. It is ready.

On the land and in the sea, the shoggoths will alter their shape to move at great speeds. — Can they fly?

The shoggoths can form limbs, eyes, and tools at will. Their bubbling and luminous masses can expand to gargantuan volumes or contract to squeeze through a keyhole.

Tekeli-Li.   Tekeli-Li.

15'

Were the mass of an avg. shoggoth was compacted, it would form about a 15' sphere. Some are larger.

How was Dyer able to escape from such a thing?

Tekeli Li...
Tekeli Li....
Tekeli Li...

Copy of photographic plate #187x aka "The Recipe"
Miskatonic University expedition 1930
by Dr. Danforth / Prof. Dyer
Bas-relief, gallery #4
Antarctic City

M.U. curator,
Fligver, has informed
me that this, along with
a good portion of the associated
research, was recently stolen
during a "break in of a
most "bizarre nature."
Must follow up!

Strange similarities to the method used by the Morato
expedition crew in 1939. Who or what taught them to
marinate penguin meat?? Did some migrate from Antarctica
to the Orkeys? What were they escaping from??

ALBINO PENGUIN AU VIN BLANC

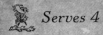

Serves 4

Foraged Rations

4 no-skin, bone-in giant albino penguin breasts
  (meat of the common chicken will do)

¼ cup vinegar

½ teaspoon each salt and pepper, plus more to taste

1 cup white wine (dry Riesling or Chardonnay), plus more if needed

4 strips bacon, chopped

3 garlic cloves, minced

1 white onion, finely chopped

1 pound portobello mushrooms, sliced

1 cup heavy cream

Chopped parsley

Prepared rice or pasta

Moneta's Preparation

Put penguin breasts in a large bowl with a mix of vinegar, salt, and pepper, then add enough white wine to cover completely. Let marinate for 3 days in a chamber of unforgiving cold, covered. If you substituted with chicken breast, skip that step and continue onward.

Pat dry the breasts with paper towels, season thoroughly with salt and pepper, set aside. Take the chopped swine flesh and sauté in a large pan for 3 minutes. Fry the garlic in the rendered fat until golden, 2 minutes. Add the onion and portobellos, and cook until bacon is crispy, about 6 minutes. Remove all from the pan.

Sear the breasts to finish the deed. Add everything again to the pan, cooking until done, about 3 to 4 minutes, turning the meat once. Add more white wine if needed and a pinch of salt. Simmer for 15 to 20 minutes, covered. Add the cream, pinch of pepper, and simmer for 4 to 5 minutes more.

Plate the breasts and pour sauce on top. Top with parsley and devour with rice or pasta.

"Penguins were the most abundant prey … With the meat (breast and thighs were the only edible parts) we made various kinds of stews and also baked breaded fillets, however it was necessary to marinate the meat before, because it had a strong wild taste. The process included washing the pieces and putting them on a big crockery pot with vinegars, salt, peppers, assorted spices, and Worcestershire sauce. We left them marinating for at least two days."

—José M. Moneta,
Four Antarctic Years in the South Orkney Islands, 1939

CURRIED FAVOR OF THE OLD ONES

They are, They shall ever be, They hunger. Let him who hath understanding, reckon the Number of the Beets, for it is a human number.

 Serves 4 of Those Who Shall Be Taken Last

Sacrificial Elements

1 teaspoon turmeric powder

½ teaspoon ground coriander

½ teaspoon salt

1 tablespoon sugar

3 tablespoons sweet curry powder

2 pounds chicken breasts

2 tablespoons unsalted butter, plus more for greasing

2 (15-ounce) cans coconut milk

2 cloves garlic, crushed

3 sweet potatoes and 3 red beets, cut into 1-inch cubes

1 medium sweet onion, cut into 1-inch pieces

Rice jasmine, cooked

The Ritual

Bring forth the lesser ceremonial bowl. In it, combine the turmeric powder, coriander, essential saltes, sugar, and curry Cain's sweet gift.

Prostrate the fowl offering in the Great Vessel of Prolonged Fever, being sure to first anoint the vessel with the Yellow Rod obtained from the Land of Lakes.

Pour within the milk of the coconut and ¾ cup of water. Raise up and reseat the fowl offering so it is not scorched.

Into this, add the small measure of the Yellow Rod, garlic, and the contents of the lesser bowl. Stir the contents until all become one.

Crosby the Egyptian will join the other cubed and many-skinned elementals. Labor again to combine.

Cover the vessel and bank the fires low for a third day, or on high for a quarter day. Patience will be rewarded. The fowl shapes should be tender when pierced. In this way, you will know it is done! Place the finished thing upon a bed of jasmine rice. Together, they shall be consumed to nourish the Names Unspeakable and their faithful.

"Staring into the rings of the Egyptian, I fall into the necessary trance..." —Ashmore's journal "rings of the Egyptian"

—Dyer and Hendrick had their theories, but now I KNOW!

The magenta rings are hypnotic! Do not stare too long.

Over a day had passed and the spell was ruined.

—More perplexed now than when I began. Appears as if they are written by different individuals — cannot find any variation in the handwriting.

—compiled and transcribed by one person?

THE FATE OF THE ELDER THINGS

What Te Must Gather

1 large eggplant, cleansed in the waters of spring

5 large eggs (from chickens, not plants—no matter what you are capable of)

$\frac{1}{2}$ cup of all-purpose flour (not flower—focus!)

1 cup filled with the oil of virgin (. . . olives)

$1\frac{1}{2}$ cups of breadcrumbs seasoned in the Mediterranean reaches

1 jar of red, red, marinara sauce (conceal your disappointment, lest you be discovered!)

The stars are ripe! Obtain the fruit of one.

Cheeses: 8 ounces of mozzarella, 4 ounces of Cheddar that is shred

$\frac{2}{3}$ cup whole milk

$\frac{1}{8}$ cup of heavily whipped cream

$\frac{1}{4}$ teaspoon each powders of garlic and onion

The Rite

Form a pseudopod into a keen blade, rise up against your former masters, and separate your victim from its top 1 to 2 inches. Now, wielding your blade-limb, slice vertically between its hideous, rigid skin. Using other limbs, spin the carcass to separate all of the internals from the shell. Small horizontal cuts may be needed at the bottom to free the succulent innards. Do not sever the bottom completely!

Widen your blade, and gleefully make four vertical cuts, roughly $\frac{1}{4}$ inch wide, through the sides of the vessel you have formed, starting $\frac{1}{2}$ inch below the neck, and to within 1 inch of the bottom.

With righteous fury and cries of "Tekeli-li!", give no quarter—but quarter and requarter the removed innards of victim.

Place these cuboids onto a parchment, and rub salt in the wounds. Allow the suffering for several minutes, then pat dry the prepared pieces.

Now form a whisk, and blend the eggs. Set these aside.

Coat each of the cuboids in the essence of the unborn fowls, and plunge them into the breadcrumb-flour mix.

The measurements are precise—why do other researchers persist in getting this wrong?

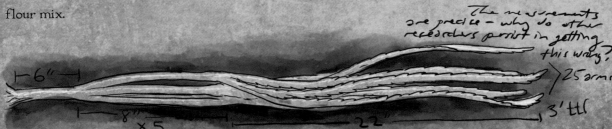

6"

8"
× 5

22

25 arms

3' ttl

Having heated the oil in a low pan, place all the pieces within and cook until they brown. Thence remove them for rest upon a new parchment.

In a small pan, place the cheeses and melt on low heat, then stir in the milk and cream. Sparing a limb, whisk patiently until smooth—then whisper the words and add in the powders.

Warm the sauce from beside the Sea.

Present the Feast of Victory!

Place the vessel upright in the center of a plate. Spill the red copiously around it with abandon. Fill the vessel with the hot, melted cheese, scatter the cubed and breaded innards around the former shell that housed them, and place a skinned slab of the star's fruit upon the neck as a mocking effigy of the once mighty—and FEAST! Dip! Ladle! Tekeli-li!

Removing the internals. No need to be clean about it.

Horizontal cuts to assist in removing the meat

Tekeli-li!

FOUL-LAFEL

 Serves to damn four unwilling victims

Tools of the Unspeakable

1 cup dried chickpeas

1 cup roughly chopped onion

2 tablespoons chopped fresh parsley

1 teaspoon each salt, cumin, and dried hot red pepper

4 cloves of garlic

1 teaspoon baking powder

4 to 6 tablespoons all-purpose flour

1 package or jar baby corn

Vegetable oil

4 pieces pita bread

Chopped tomato, diced onion and green bell pepper, and pickled turnips, for garnish

Tahini sauce, for drizzling

The Corrupting

I've seen 'em do it. They take the chickpeas an' drown 'em in a big tub of cold water. They leave 'em there overnight, and then drain 'em like it was nothin'.

I can't barely think about the next part. They got this thing, with a steel blade. It spins, and makes a noise like an angry swarm ah bees. They put the chickpeas and some onion along with all kinds spices and garlic and blend 'em all up.

After some dancin' around, they sprinkle the baking powder and flour into the mess they made, and give it a couple more whirrs. How they keep it from being sticky, I don't know. Maybe more flour? It all goes in a large bowl they stick in the chiller for a couple hours.

Now they got a big pot boilin' and they're throwin' in baby corn! Aw, jeez—it never had no chance! Salt in there too. I ain't never seen this kinda cruelty. It's over quick. Maybe 5 minutes. They take 'em out, all tender-like, and lay 'em on a towel like they was just goin' down for a nap.

Back to the bowl. They make these kinda balls out of it. Maybe twenty or so.

They acquire a deep bowl like they got in Chinatown, but with three inches of hot oil inna bottom, think it was heated to 375 degrees F. They're smart. They test just one. Fryin' the ball for a few minutes onna side, waitin' til golden brown. If it falls apart, they put more flour to it. When they got it right, they fry 'em all. They come out a golden brown, and they lay 'em back on the towel to drain.

After that is the worst. They stuff the flat bread things with a couple of those balls, all garnished up with tomatoes an' onion, green peppers, pickled turnips, and the baby corn cut in strips. These they leave hangin' out and I swear I saw 'em wigglin' as they ate 'em! it was awful. All drizzled with that pale sauce. . . . Why'd you send me here?! Why!? If you knew. . . . You gotta bring the others. Come quick. I think they see me!

My dear friend, Prof. Dykes informed me that law authorities from Midway had been directed to him over the matter of 5 curious symbols that were found to have been recently branded onto Mr. Warren's body. This is how I first heard of the case.

—— the symbols branded onto Kyle Warren's person. He felt no pain and had no memory of receiving them

bottom of left foot
sigil of the moon beasts

nape of the neck
?

Center of the back, btw the shoulder blades
this one I've seen before—in Carter's journal, the sigil of Shub-Niggurath

right tricep, just above the elbow
?

1" below the navel
Symbol of the "burrowing ones"

So reminiscent of creatures from a dream. They spoke to me of other worlds. Invited me to stay. They were horrid but I was not frightened.

The cowl, or bell was like that of a jellyfish

feelers, flat on one side, like a slug

I must see the Warren autopsy report. Why won't they return my calls?
contact R. Blackstone
MTPD

SIDES

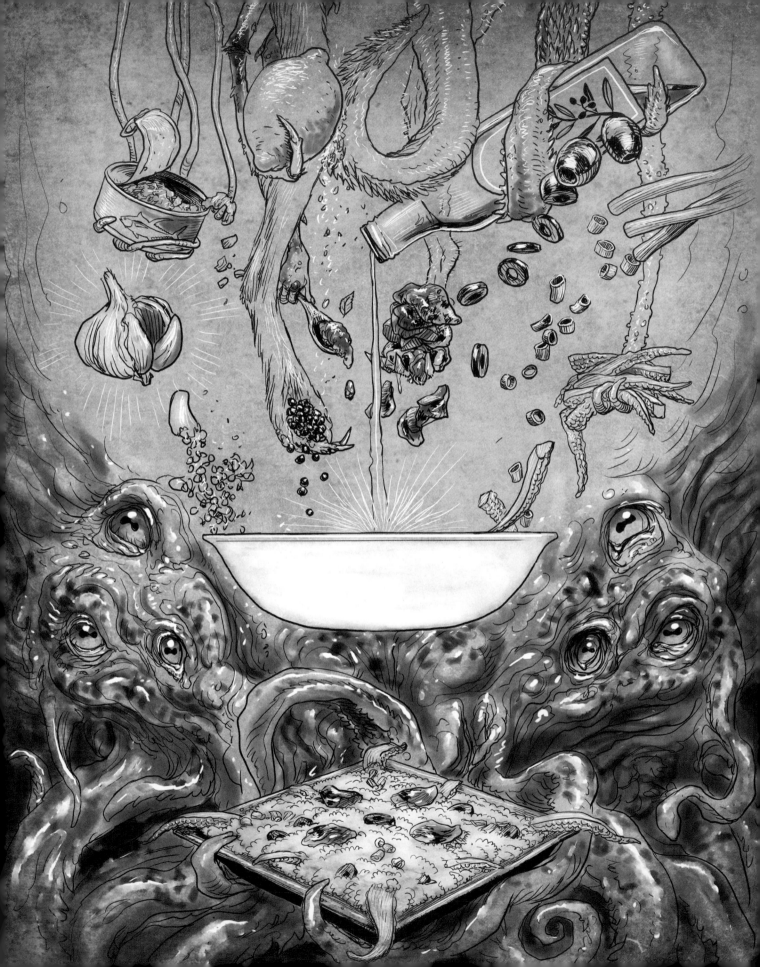

CTHUS-KOOS

 Serves Four, and the Dreamer

Rise and Obtain

1 teaspoon kosher salt, plus more to taste

½ package or jar baby corn, sliced carefully, quartered lengthwise

1 cup Israeli couscous

4 ounces tuna, cooked, drained, and flaked

1 teaspoon lemon zest

¼ cup olive oil

¼ cup pitted black olives, chopped into ringlets

1 tablespoon capers, drained

1 cup pesto

¼ cup diced roasted red peppers

1 clove garlic, minced

1 teaspoon freshly ground black pepper

¼ cup freshly squeezed lemon juice

1 cup chopped scallions

When t the Stars Are Right

Upon awakening, make thee a representation of the sea with the prescribed full portion of salt and water in a middling-sized pot. Boil this, and add the corn tendrils until they soften and writhe, one twelfth hour. Remove them and most of the moisture that clings to them.

Thence, in the medium vessel over flame, add the couscous to boiling water. The ratio is one to four, as it was before R'lyeh sank beneath the waves, as it shall be when it rises again! Cover this, and let it simmer as My kin do in our tomb, for one quarter-hour. After this interval, drain and set by.

A large stone or metal concavity is needed now. In it, thou wilt place the sea offering, the grated skin of the citrus, the oil and flesh of olive—caper with abandon now, for the time is near—the sauce of pestilent green, the fiery red peppers, half of the corn tendrils, garlic, additional salts, and black spice. Into this pour the still-hot grains and stir, as when I visit thy sleeping mind. Set this by for a short time, say one quarter-hour, stirring between the aeons.

When thy time to serve arrives, infuse the offering with the juice and the green rings, garnish at strange angles with the remaining corn tendrils. A pinch of the native salt to top. Feast in My name, and revels shall be thine when I wake!

THE UNKNOWN KA'SQUASH

 Serves Four Who Have Been Warned

The Path

1 large spaghetti squash

Salt and pepper

2 tablespoons brown sugar

2 tablespoons extra virgin olive oil

¼ cup fresh basil leaves, finely sliced

1 clove garlic, finely chopped

¼ cup grated Parmesan, plus more for topping

2 ripe tomatoes, halved

¾ cup shredded mozzarella

The Journey

Barzai instructed me in the preliminary 375 degrees F. In half we struck the sacrificial squash, and removed the innards even as we climbed. His eyes gleamed feverishly as he bade me season them with the the light and dark to taste. He placed both halves of the husk face down in the high-sided pan he had brought for the purpose. From a single cup, he poured water into the pan, and chanted for near an hour as they roasted. Cooked through and tender he said they had to be. He was wise in the way of such things, and I followed as well as I could, though he scrambled madly ahead.

He was screaming at me from a place I could not reach. His voice was wild, "Flip them! Flip them and cast the brown sweetness upon them! Let the pale vapor escape!" The temperature was dropping steadily now, and my patience rewarded as I allowed them to fully cool.

His hand appeared in a claw above me, making raking motions and pointing at the husks. His willing servant, I shredded the sweet meat of the squash into long noodles. When I'd done this deed and the skins were loosed and empty, he waved his hand like an upended cup. I had studied closely by him, and took this to mean the liquids were of no consequence, so it was discarded.

His voice was thunderous and wild, and I was verging on terror. I prepared the greased pan as he commanded, and mixed well in a bowl the raked flesh, the olive's oils, the herbs, and all the other seasonings as well as the strange white granules of Par Mexan he'd brought.

A voice that was not Barzai's slithered around me. Drawn inexorably to some hellish will, I made portions of four on the sheet, cloven red hemispheres of tomato I pressed into these and the shredded white substance I scattered with abandon upon them! Continuing in my labors, I festooned the creations with additional white granules of Par Mezan. The temperature rose (again to 375) and these abominations returned once more to the heat for half an hour. The offering, all a-bubble and browning is complete.

Wise Barzai would want us to feast, that it not go to cold waste . . .

THE SIDE DISH NOT TO BE NAMED

Cast

2 tablespoons olive oil

¾ cup pearl onions

¾ cup spinach

⅓ cup bok choy, cut to thin strips

Kosher salt and black pepper to taste

Pinch of nutmeg

1 tablespoon all purpose flour

½ cup milk

¾ cup shredded Colby-Jack cheese

Recital

In a skillet heat one measure of oil

Take thee care it should not boil

Add onions, cook till edges brown

And to translucence closer

Add spinach, bok choy, salt, and pepper,

Nutmeg too, till spinach wilts like skin of leper

Remove from heat and set aside

Repeat first step once over

Whisk in flour and cook until bubbling

Add in milk slowly and continue troubling

Remove from heat, add cheese, mix 'til melted

To this the green, and salt kosher

Add this to the other feast

Face-to-face with what released

Unmask now, if thou may

Tis past the time for poseur

Variation from the Ashmore Journal, but his source is unknown.

The Sigil of Hastur

Carcassonne

O. Baer writes of a dish that I can only assume to be the very same. He mentions that spinach is the closest thing, in both taste and texture, to a crimson plant that grows in great patches along the shores of the Demhe. It is necessary to substitute for, I think, obvious reasons.

Speaking with O. Baer, he says that his source was a 16th c. text on the culinary traditions of the Aude phin in southern France.

When I arrived at
the sock, they
offered me a hot
bowl of the spicy
mixture and a sealed
jar for the long
journey ahead.

They do seem
welcoming to
outsiders.

Dark urges consumed
my thoughts —

I was a great
worm, consuming
all manner of life,
from those that
burrowed to those
that scurried and
on to those that
lumbered.
Devouring man
and city of man.

TCHO-TCHO CHOW-CHOW

 Serves Mankind (about 6 cups)

Ingredients

1 head (of cauliflower)

2 small yellow onions, diced

1 cup distilled white vinegar

1 cup fresh lemon juice

2 teaspoons kosher salt

½ cup sugar

½ teaspoon dried crushed red pepper

2 yellow bell peppers, diced

2 red bell peppers, diced

8 banana peppers, diced

2 tablespoons minced fresh thyme

1 ounce Zayda's horseradish

Special for You

Take up a large cauldron, and place within the white brainy mass. Perform the Rite of Execration, and add onions, turned wine, bitter juices, salt, sugar, and the red spice to one cup of boiling water. Perform the Rite of A Thousand Dzhow.

Let this simmer under a lesser heat, until the sacred mixture is reduced over the course of perhaps an hour. Stir in the colored peppers—they put the wary at ease, being recognizable to local palates. Stir for perhaps one-twelfth hour, then take from the flame and let stand one-half hour.

Now the thyme is right, and also the devil-spice. Mix these in immediately before offering to Those Who Wait, that they may serve to greatest effect. The *dʒhow-dʒhow* may be stored many days, but refresh the last two items each time, or its potence may wane.

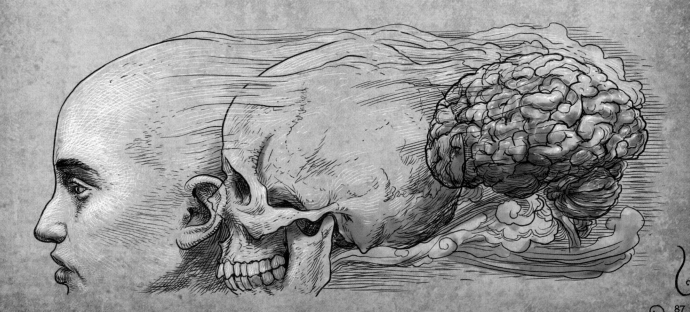

BREAKFAST

THE MUESLI OF ERICH ZANN

 Serves an ensemble of four who seek to keep the hungering dawn at bay

Notes

1⅓ cups Haferflocken | avoine roulante | rolled oats

1 cup Kokosmilch | lait de coco | milk (whole, coconut, or almond)

4 Großmutter Schmied Apfel | pomme Grany | Granny Smith apples

1⅓ cups Naturjoghurt | yogourt insipide | vanilla or plain 4% fat yogurt

¼ cup gehobelte Mandeln | amandes en tranches | sliced almonds

½ cup getrocknete Erdbeeren | fraises pas humides | dried strawberries

½ cup getrocknete Blaubeeren | myrtilles pas humides | dried blueberries

¼ cup Sonnenblumenkerne | graines de fleur du soleil | sunflower seeds

4 teaspoons Honig | miel | honey

Pandemonium

At first, I thought the old man simply eccentric, and perhaps a bit senile. I would pass him in the kitchen, always in the mornings, and sometimes find he had left his oats to soak what seemed overlong, nearly 10 minutes. Once I reached for the bowl to tip some of the milk out and save him ruining them—but he surprised me then, his bony fingers flying for the bowl to stay me. The look of anger and fear that crossed his visage I can neither explain, nor forget.

He was mute, and so he waved at me scrawled notes in egregious French, clumsily translated from his German. I could not tell if the apples were to be half shredded, for some reason unfathomable, or if half the apples should be treated thus. Grudgingly he showed me when I imposed. Two of the apples he grated very coarsely, adding them to the oats. The other two he sliced to slivers, his knife flying like the bow of some mad violinist. When I thought the slivers could be no thinner or more numerous, with a series of savage chops, he halved them. Much of this went into the oats as well.

Glancing furtively at the cupboard, he reached for the yogurt. When I made to try the latch to see if there was something within that he needed—he flew at me again, pulling me frantically back toward the old kitchen chairs. He made me sit, and I watched him in fascination as he poured his previous work into the thick yogurt, sprinkling slices of almond, curiously lifeless berries of various kind, and seeds. Covering the bowl as I wished to cover my ears, he shook this with a ferocious cacophony I cannot describe, or banish from my memory.

When the fit that had seized him passed, he opened the great bowl. With a mad zeal he drizzled honey upon what was there, and subsiding, artfully placed the remainder of the sliced almonds and slivered apples. Skirting the cupboard warily, he set this to chill for the next morning, and retired.

At dawn, I arose; and not hearing him bustling about—I went to the shabby kitchen in that forgotten house. The cupboard stood open; and of the man and his notes all that remained—was the muesli of Erich Zann.

So many discordant notes, forming a perfect medley

That is not bread
which can eternal fry
And with strange toppings
open the Eye

I have spent all my life
pursuing those things from
which men would flee. From
which they would recoil and writhe
as would an earthworm from
the searing point of magnified
sunlight. Envious of those
who have witnessed those
horrific wonders, those things
that now linger and taunt their
every waking moment, I shall
continue to pursue the knowledge
and feast upon the secrets.

It is a delicate operation to keep
the eyes intact!

VEGEMITEY CTHULHU

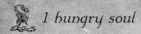 *1 hungry soul*

To Be Sacrificed That He May Come Forth

2 slices pumpernickel

2 teaspoons unsalted butter

2 tablespoons of Vegemite

2 cups bean sprouts

2 large eggs

Wake the Dreamer!

Rend the center of the bread slabs with voids of dire shape. Brush upon the slabs a bit of the yellow and black-umber substances.

Maintain your vigil—and in a vessel devoid of one dimension, melt a bit more of the butter and place the black slabs. Scatter about half the sprouts and stir these throughout with soft susserations.

Break open the fowl egg, and pour forth into the void! Twice you will do thus, one into each eye.

Maintain the intensity of the medium. After the passing of two counts sixty, turn the slabs and their fowl contents over, and brush again upon them the pastes. When the yoke is set upon all Mankind— yield, and serve garnished with a beard of the tendrils untouched by flame.

YOGASH THE GRUEL

The Line of Descent

1 cup rice, black as the void

2 pinches salt

2 cups holy water

1 cup milk, pure and undiluted

2 teaspoons sugar, raw and unrefined

½ teaspoon vanilla extract

The Consuming Ebon Ink

Alabaster Glaze

The Inheritance

Scion of the Blackness Between and Before, line of
The First, heed me if you would feast as did your fathers!
These are the steps upon the path set by Shaurash-ho!

Cleanse you the ebon grains, and drown them under a black moon. Bathe them again after sunrise and before putting them to the cauldron. Note well that they should be wholly drained before proceeding.

Throw one pinch of salt over your left shoulder, and the other in an iron cauldron. Bathe the rice once more in the sanctified waters, and set all to boil. When the bubbles arise and break, bank the flame low.

Cover them now from the open sky. The tomb lid should allow no air within, nor any vapor to escape!

After one third-hour, gift the feast with the milk, sugar, and vanilla extract. Set aside the tomb lid, and allow all within to stir.

After a further one-third hour, the shining black-purple sheen of unlife should stare back from the depths. To your purpose and humor, infuse so many tears of the Ebon ink as pleases you.

You will taste the yield of your labor and know success when tooth and tender balance!

Serve in a black or copper bowl. Forego the Rune in Alabaster if those who feast are to be as the wild kin; or inscribe it to float above your yield if that heritage is to be concealed. Complements of fresh butter or cream gathered under cover of darkness from surrounding fields is appropriate, if you are careful.

Stay among them. Walk unknown. All shall come to you, in the end.

As always, choose your protective rune with care! Devour the gruel while seated facing the closed door to the room – this is most necessary for the rune to work. Do not attempt this in a room with more than one entrance!

heavy cream ——— butter ——— brown sugar

GREAT OLD BUNS

 Serves the Outer Gods, and makes 12 buns

What Lies Within

¾ cup warm water

1 tablespoon active dry yeast

3 cups all-purpose flour

1 tablespoon instant powdered milk

¼ cup sugar

½ teaspoon salt

1 egg

1 egg white

3 tablespoons unsalted butter

¾ cup dried cranberries

1 teaspoon cinnamon

1 egg yolk with 2 tablespoons water

The Seal

½ cup confectioners' powdered sugar

¼ teaspoon vanilla extract

2 teaspoons milk

Elder sign

Order of Teeth.

Cth.

Nyarl.

Dagon

Burrowers

The Yellow Sign

Hastur

Long Tradesm.

Yitzilitt fragments — Princeton RBSC

The Tombs

To fashion the oubliettes, begin when Sol is well risen—and none of the homes of the inimical look down upon the Earth.

Combine thee the warmed and purified water with the leavening yeast. Five minutes under the Standing Blades of Mik'zing should suffice.

To this add the flour, dried milk, sugar, salt, egg, and egg white. Observe this order, or the ward may not hold!

Take up the artifice, having girded it with the Hook of Dough, and allow it for one-sixth hour to slowly commingle what has gone before. Now is the time to add the softened yellow fat, the dried cranberries, and the sacred umber cinnamon spice. Maintain the labor again for one-sixth hour.

Prepare a vessel whose walls have been made slick, to prevent them slipping free before the oubliettes can begin to set. Place the doughy mass in the vessel thus prepared, and cover it well. The entombed shall strive against what you have prepared for them. In about 1 hour, when the nuclear chaos from which they arose and to which we shall banish them has grown to twice its initial size, take this and smite it onto a surface blanketed in the dust of flour. Cover it quickly! Abide one-sixth hour.

You must separate the Entombed lest they combine their efforts and undo yours. Rend the primal mass into twelfths. They will take on a rounded shape if you will it. Place each of these onto a metallic plane prepared as the vessel was previously, with butter. The consecrated fats will prevent them gaining any purchase which could leave them a path of escape. Cover them again, and witness—again shall their struggles give rise to a second doubling when 40 minutes have fled!

When this has come to pass, brush upon the surface of each cell a mixture of the yolk and water. With a blade blessed against them, inscribe lightly the runes that shall seal them within. Into each cut, dust the sacred umber spice.

Now they will be unable to further oppose thee. Seal them within the kiln at 375th degree, abiding one-quarter to one-third of an hour—no more! Remove them at once, to cool upon a mesh of metal.

The Final Seal is made in the Old Way. Combine the crystalline sugar, vanilla extract, and milk. Imprint this over the sigils you have engraved.

Carry these rites down the generations, for We shall not be upon the Earth when next They awaken!

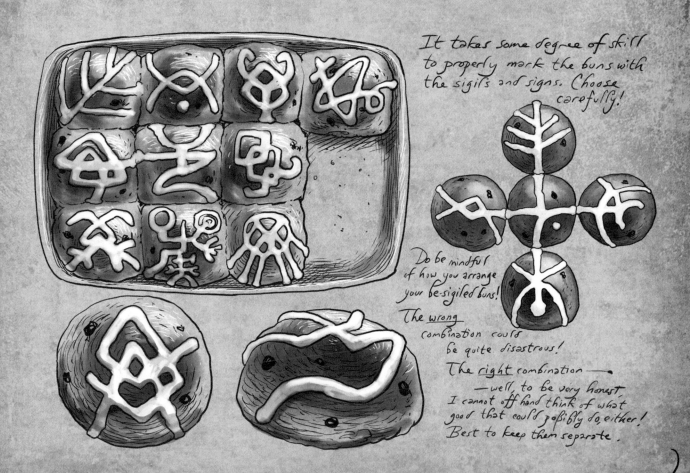

It takes some degree of skill to properly mark the buns with the sigils and signs. Choose carefully!

Do be mindful of how you arrange your be-sigiled buns!

The wrong combination could be quite disastrous!

The right combination —

—well, to be very honest, I cannot off hand think of what good that could possibly do, either! Best to keep them separate.

They say that an unfed
Deep One will, over an
unknown period of time,
continue to shrink - I think
feeding on its own matter.
I do wonder just how small
they can get and if their brains
retain the knowledge, intelligence, and
function of their former selves.

THE OATS OF DAGON

 Makes 16 squares

First Sacraments

2 cups rolled oats

1½ cups all-purpose flour

12 tablespoons unsalted butter, melted

1 teaspoon cinnamon

¼ teaspoon salt

½ teaspoon baking soda

¼ teaspoon nutmeg

1 cup light brown sugar, packed

Second Sacraments

1 cup applesauce

½ cup crushed almonds

6 strips cooked bacon, crumbled

Third Sacrament

1 teaspoon powdered sugar

The First Oath

Fire the kiln to 350°F.

Stir, Oh Father of Grains, the souls of those who have taken the First Sacraments! When the water of life is even in them, take and set aside Thy Chosen in the Cup of Dagon's Oats!

The Second Oath

May those who remain, be pressed firmly into service to thee upon the baking vessel, slick with fat.

Subject to the heat for 15 minutes. When the Sacred Grain has formed a crust we shall remove them from the kiln, and spread upon them the Second Sacraments!

The Third Oath

The Chosen shall lay upon them and be anointed with the Third Sacrament. When this is done, dress them again in the saved cup of the First Oath, take them again to the fires. Give them respite after one quarter hour—no more. Watch them carefully, as even this could be more than is needful.

Separate them as it pleases, the Four Angles should be right.

CHILDREN'S MEALS

CULTISTS IN ROBES

 Serves to initiate six of the next generation

Components

12 breakfast sausages
Biscuit or croissant roll dough
Yellow Spice, Scarlet Sauce, or Sauce of Bhar-bek-hue

The Initiation

Demonstrate for the neonates the use of the blade, unless their skill is already advanced and they may be entrusted with its use.

In the middle of the sausage-effigy, pierce and cut lengthwise to the end. Cleave these two sections again at least twice, lengthwise again.

Cut a thin slice of dough for the robe. It should be of a length slightly greater than that of the sausages.

Enrobe the cut sausages, pinching at the uncut side of the sausage to form the cowl, and wrapping the rest, loosely at the bottom where the cuts were made.

Pierce each effigy with a pair of small stakes, forming an X in the mid-section just above the cuts.

Begin the Trial by Flame, and bake these into upright members of the Order, splaying the cut portions with the blade if necessary to nestle them in the tempering wells. The preheated 375th degree will complete their trial at the thirteenth minute. You will know they are ready when the bubbling whispers are present and their robes have taken a golden hue as the power of the ritual suffuses them!

They may be further anointed with the Yellow Spice, the Scarlet Sauce of the Hunt, or the Sauce of Bhar'bek-hue.

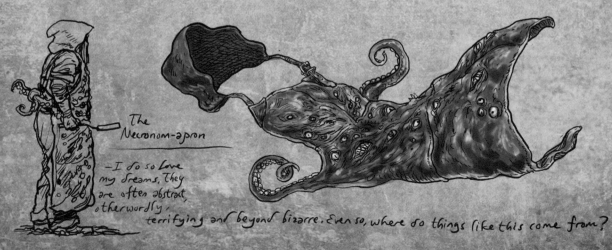

The Necronom-apron
—————————

—I do so love my dreams. They are often abstract, otherwordly, terrifying and beyond bizarre. Even so, where do things like this come from?

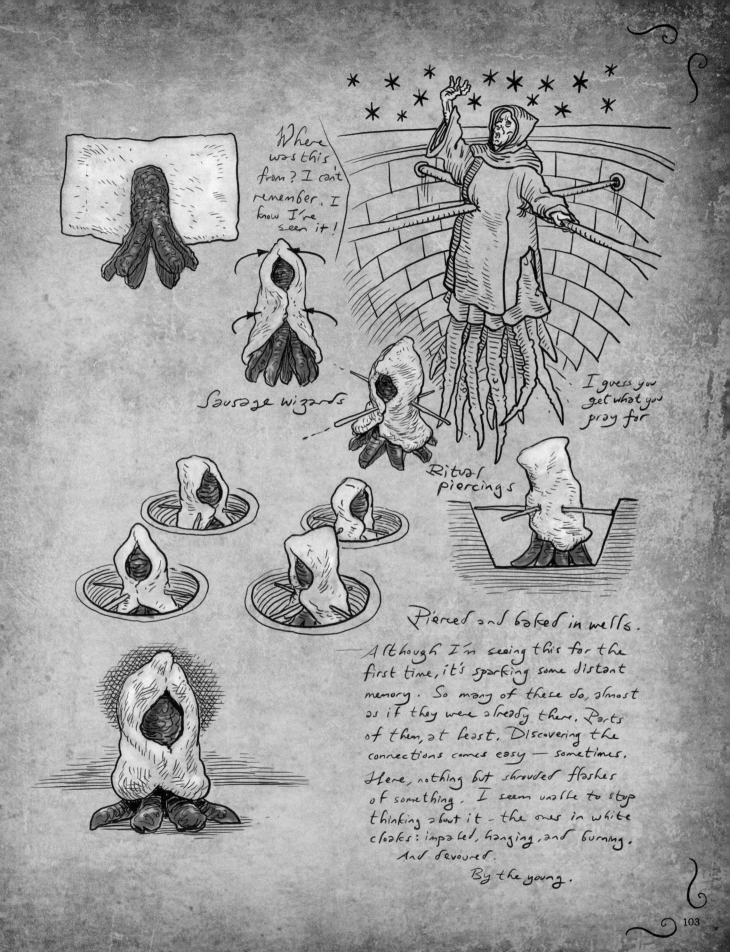

Where was this from? I can't remember. I know I've seen it!

Sausage wizards

I guess you get what you pray for

Ritual piercings

Pierced and baked in wells.

— Although I'm seeing this for the first time, it's sparking some distant memory. So many of these do, almost as if they were already there. Parts of them, at least. Discovering the connections comes easy — sometimes.

Here, nothing but shrouded flashes of something. I seem unable to stop thinking about it - the ones in white cloaks: impaled, hanging, and burning. And devoured.

By the young.

The opening of their mouths

Do not conceal the serpents within the mass! Allow them to writhe free!

YIGGY PUDDING

 Serves 8 wriggling children

Gribblies

1 (3.9-ounce) package dark-hued Caco Pudding for the Out of Time

2 cups cold milk

2 ounces dark-hued fragments of cacao for sprinkling

Crimson Orbs of Maraschin-Yoh

16 Gui-mai Wyrms

The Churning Mass

Bring the Chosen of Yig a large bowl. See that the child pours in the entirety of the dry contents, and allow this one to add the cold milk of the cow. Assist with the mixing if necessary.

When all is smooth, allow it to sit and thicken for a short time, about 5 minutes. Then hand the child that dark matter which is to be sprinkled, and the Crimson Orbs of Maraschin-Yoh. See that these are mixed in well.

Divide the result evenly between eight cups or disks.

The Elder should take up an obsidian blade, and cut slits along the end of the worms to open their mouths. Insert a pair of these into each mass of darkness so that most of the serpent remains visible. Place a few more Crimson Orbs on top of the serving so they also are not hidden. Refrigerate one hour before serving, the worms are best consumed while torpid. Over time, the child will absorb them, and under your guidance grow wise in the Ways.

LOVECRAFT MACARONI AND CHEESE

 Serves 6 to 8 Dark Young

The Nourishments Need Just

2 boxes Kraft Macaroni & Cheese

2 cups milk

2 tablespoons unsalted butter

1 cup shredded mozzarella

2½ cups shredded extra-sharp Cheddar

1½ (12-ounce) packages spinach fettuccine

1 cup frozen peas

½ teaspoon salt

¼ teaspoon freshly ground black pepper

The Offering to the Dark Young

Those adept with the Kraft shall know the Way, as it is written on the tablets. Prepare as the tradition demands, though you may enhance in the late stage, after the powders have been subsumed, with the white and yellow filaments.

In a pan wide and low, boil water and spread the dried husks which shall bloom into the grasping green tendrils. Be certain of two things: their reach through space is sufficient that they be not curled upon themselves; and that they are removed "with the teeth" intact, or *al dente* as the Mediterranean would say. Again, the traditional way will be divined from the packaging. Leave them not overlong, and rinse with the cool water as it is written upon the cask where they were held. Heed the ancient ways!

The Emerald Orbs shall be removed from the icy darkness and put directly into seas a'boil. These too remove while the colour and firmness remain. Time and the wheel of the Stars are inimical—take now no respite and remain vigilant!

When all is in readiness, leave the elements in the separate summoning vessels. Upon each receptacle prepared for the Dark Young, lay a bed of the Yellow Mass. Upon this scatter pullulately the fell green tendrils, and upon them profligately decorate the Emerald Orbs.

Repeat this such that a second dimensional layer superpose the first, ending with a lesser mound of the mac and cheese, and topped by a scattering of peas so that all is a heaving mass, wild in shape and riot in turn.

The pale crystal and ebon flakes may now be scattered atop.

The seeming writhe and twist of the clashing and conjoining elements shall bring delight and sustenance as they grow. Watch over them well, and delight in what delights them.

SHOGG-POCKETS

Serves Four Not Yet Grown to Full Size

Whatch' ll Need

Butter

Dough of Pizzah

Tomato Sauce with meatballs

Slices of Pepperoni, thick and quartered

Shredded mozzarella and Cheddar

The Shape of Things to Yun

On a flat metal sheet which you buttered up good, shape some raw dough into a shapeless shape. All the parts of the shape should be wide enough for what comes next.

Spread some of the beast's red blood around the inside, leaving some clear space 'round the edges. A few of the small meaty globes should get in there, scattered about.

Put a few chunks of meat pyramids in amongst the sauce, and scatter both kinds of shreds, yellow and white on top.

This bit is fiddly, and there's different ways yeh can do it, but make a shapeless shape like the first one, a li'l smaller. Lay that on top, and squish an' pinch the edges all together good and proper. If some of the pyramids or globes poke through a bit—that's good! That's fine. It'll be fine. . . . They gotta breathe a bit.

Make as many more as yeh need. Put 'em in the hot oven, 'bout 375 degrees F, for maybe a quarter hour, dependin' on how big yeh made 'em.

When they's golden, bubbly, and done, put 'em on plates—an' see who eats who first!

Imperfections in the process seem to breed more interesting results.

DESSERTS

TO SUMMON NYARLATHOTAPIOCA

 Serves the Outer Gods, but . . . should sate 4 adult ~~morsels~~ mortals.

To Be Sacrificed That He May Come Forth

3 cups whole milk

½ cup chronally accelerated tapioca beads

½ cup white sugar

¼ teaspoon salt

2 eggs, beaten severely

Extract from vanilla one half teaspoon of its essence, make it pray you don't need more

¼ cup pomegranate seeds

¼ cup blackberry jam

One dozen flayed red grapes

Invocation of the Thousand-Formed One

In the vessel of the Satyr-god, heat the milk of the bovine, the beads of Ta'pio-kha, and all of the Hoary Crystals of Disparate Nature. Patiently boil this, and scald not the forming chaos. Bring the flame low, and stir until one-twelfth hour has passed.

Whisk the goblet of hot milk mixture into the beaten fowl spawn, slowly (so slowly . . .).

When all is blasphemously conjugated, bring the result an ironically gentle simmer over medium-low heat; and stir just a while longer. Patience is our watchword. When the chaos can thickly crawl the back of the Shining Implement of Concavity, quench the flame.

Introduce now the extract and the blood-red seeds. Fold in the black-purple jam into the Chaos. It is a good sign when a ribbon forms in the formless, but it is not needful if such does not appear. Place in a pleasing way the skinless grapes. Let them be subsumed.

The Thousand-Formed One may be served hot if the time is short or the need is great. With cold patience of hours, so may It also be served. You will know the way by the Whispers in Darkness, if thou knowest how to listen.

The seeds will sink
to the bottom.

One should
employ great
patience and a
sharp blade for
the skinning!

Sometimes the
pudding stares
back.

The blades. The spinning blades. The ancestors
must have toiled patiently without such a device.

"At least when never in 3 dimensions," says Mr. Moore.

114

YOGSICLES

 Serves the 8 (and the Key)

Summoning Components

8 round ice molds

2½ cups blueberries or blackberries

2 tablespoons agave syrup

2 cups 4% fat vanilla yogurt

8 round 6-inch rods

The Invocation

Having obtained the globular summoning crypts, open them in preparation.

Blend in a machine the blue-black globes until paradox is achieved. There should be the smoothness of continuity, but also the chaos of raw matter.

In a metallic vessel, pour this blend and add the sweet nectar. Gently combine this with the white yogurt which represents the negative void between spaces. It should swirl with the wheeling of a thousand galaxies. Contemplate your insignificance as you gaze at the ribbons of dark and light.

Into the lower half of each globe, pour the result. Encapsulate these then with the upper halves of the spheres. Pour the remains carefully into an amorphous plastic bag with one corner pierced. Use this to fill the top halves of the spheres through the portal each contains. Tap each gently with a large rod or spoon, then fill further any voids thus revealed. Now insert the lesser rods into the spheres.

Place in the cold of space and time, freezing them into the proper configuration. He Who is the Gate and the Key Whereby The Spheres Meet should fully manifest by the morn.

Iä! Iä Yog-Sothoth!

MOON-BEAST PIES

Send forth a slave with a small ruby to trade for these.

Serves Nyarlathotep, Mnomquah, and a dozen friends

Pies

8 tablespoons unsalted butter, softened

1 cup sugar

1 large egg

1 cup evaporated milk

1 teaspoon vanilla extract

2 cups all-purpose flour

½ teaspoon salt

1½ teaspoons baking soda

½ cup unsweetened cocoa powder

½ teaspoon baking powder

Marshmallow Jissing

8 tablespoons unsalted butter, softened

1 cup confectioners' sugar

½ teaspoon vanilla extract

1 cup marshmallow crème or fluff

Viscera

1 (12-ounce) package spaghetti

1 (3-ounce) package strawberry Jell-O

1 cup strawberry jam

Commands and Labor

For the pies: Stoke the Punishment Kiln to the 400th degree F.

In a large vessel, force the conjoining of 8 tablespoons butter and the sugar, followed swiftly by the egg, evaporated milk, and vanilla extract.

In a fresh vessel, do the same with the flour, salt, baking soda, cocoa, and baking powder.

Now—meld the two, thoroughly and patiently. This forms the dough.

From a height, allow the dough to plunge onto a greased metallic tray by generous rounded spoonfuls. Leave the span of a (human) child's hand between dollops. We don't want them spreading and joining again.

The central feelers of the Moon-beast are sucked into the head, bringing the food to an inner, circular mouth, ringed with round, white crushing teeth. No dissection has ever been performed, but when they're dropped from a great height, their blooded masses burst open.

Bake these for 6 to 8 minutes, until firm when pressed.

Allow to cool at least 1 hour before spreading the marshmallow ichor.

To create the ichor: Combine 8 tablespoons butter with confectioners' sugar, vanilla extract, and the moon cloud essence. Labor ceaselessly until smooth!

Crack the yellow pasta stalks in twain into a large pot of boiling water infused with the essence of Jell-O until quite soft.

Assemble confection of our folk by spreading 2 tablespoonfuls of filling on the flat side of a moon crust, add radially symmetrical scatterings of pastoid tendrils, and a spoonful of the red-pink jam off-center on the filling, and finally capping with another oblate hemisphere of moon crust. Low and mocking laughter is appropriate.

Serve!

The Moon-beasts appear to have a skeletal structure but are able to change their shape—to absorb or lengthen their 4 limbs—and squeeze their great masses through openings as small as the end of their twitching snouts, from which their writhing feelers protrude.

Keep our feline allies somewhere close by when preparing

JOE SLATER'S IN-BREAD PUDDING

 Serves an intelligence from another star, and 12 waking humans

What is Sent

Whiskey Sauce

8 tablespoons unsalted butter

¼ cup bourbon

1 cup sugar

2 tablespoons water (or more whiskey)

¼ teaspoon nutmeg

Dash of salt

1 large egg

Red food coloring

Pudding

3 tablespoons unsalted butter, softened

2 loaves French or Italian bread

1 cup raisins

2 teaspoons cinnamon

3 large eggs

4 cups whole milk

2 cups sugar

2 tablespoons vanilla extract

But Ferorean Icing

1½ cups confectioners' sugar

½ teaspoon vanilla extract

8 tablespoons unsalted butter

1 tablespoon whipping cream

What Spirits Possessed Him?

On the first night his fits started, the prisoner raged, demanding various things before he'd talk. He melted butter over low heat in a heavy saucepan. He was stir crazy, he sloshed in his spirit with the rest of the sauce materials, except the egg and colour. All this he blended until the sugar melted. We took the heat off him then, but he went at the egg like it done him wrong, beating at it as it went in. It was all together then, and he set the mixture back over a medium heat and just simmered in his cell, almost gentle. The plot thickened a minute later, but didn't curdle. We all watched uneasily over the night.

What Demon Drove This?

On the second night, he spread butter over a large glass baking dish and maniacally cut bread into ½-inch slices. He compulsively arranged the slices almost upright into tightly spaced rows into the baking pan, scattering raisins and half the cinnamon between the slices of bread, eyes wild.

He raved for a large bowl, in which he whisked eggs and milk until they were a froth. Sugar, vanilla, and the rest of the cinnamon went in next. Exhausted, he poured the mixture over the bread and rested for an hour—then suddenly lunged at the pan and submerged the bread repeatedly, as if to drown it. He raved about the pre-existence of the 375th degree F. To see where this lead, we baked his pan for 1 hour as he demanded. He said the signs would be puffed and brown—and he was right. We gave him what whiskey spirits he'd prepared from last night to calm him, but he poured much of it over the pan! We let him cool off for most of an hour.

What Spread before His Fevered Mind

It was clear he neared the end. We attached the shocking device. In a gentle voice not his own he told us to mix the powder, extract, and butter. The pace of his raving varied, but smoothed out after a short while. He asked for cream and continued to beat on at a medium pace for a minute more.

His last act was to spread this product of his ravings over his earlier work. He'd mixed a few drops of blood into the last of his whisky sauce. And piped what he called an Elder Sign into the frosting with a straw. With a shaking hand, he poured the rest of his spirit into the work, his eyes flared open and . . . and it was finished. His life, and something else, fled. Free.

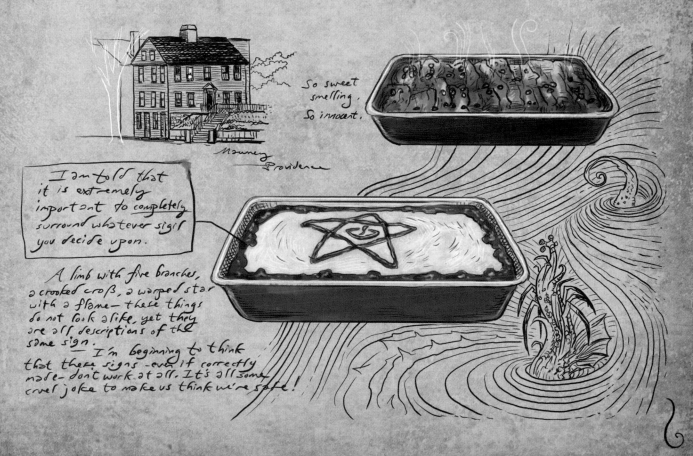

So sweet smelling. So innocent.

Newney Providence

I am told that it is extremely important to completely surround whatever sigil you decide upon.

A limb with five branches, a crooked cross, a warped star with a flame—these things do not look alike, yet they are all descriptions of the same sign. I'm beginning to think that these signs—even if correctly made—don't work at all. It's all some cruel joke to make us think we're safe!

THE MOUNDS OF TINDALOS

 Serves 6 to 8 Who Would Brave the Angles of Time

What Must Be Used

Chocolate Cake

4 tablespoons unsalted butter, melted

1 cup each all-purpose flour and sugar

1 large egg

1 teaspoon vanilla extract

½ cup baking cocoa

1 teaspoon each baking soda and baking powder

1 bag dark chocolate morsels

2 cups shredded coconut, sweetened

2 pinches of salt

Canola oil

Pudding

1 cup sugar

½ cup baking cocoa

¼ cup cornstarch

½ teaspoon salt

4 cups milk

2 tablespoons unsalted butter

2 teaspoons vanilla extract

To Make the Aversion

In a large unangled container, thrash together the butter and sugar until a strange lightness abides in them, and then add The Egg—and achieve the same, followed by The Extract.

In another angleless form, whisk the flour, cocoa, baking soda, baking powder, and salt; and then add these to the creamed mixture—in parts!—combining thoroughly after each addition. Stir in one cup of hot water until blended.

To bring the pudding into this world: In a large pan, round and heavy, combine the sugar, cocoa, cornstarch, and salt. Patiently add the milk. Over a modest flame, bring this to a boil, stirring for two counts sixty. Extinguish the fire, and stir in the butter and vanilla evenly.

Mist the Oil of K'no-lah upon the inner space of the artifice constructed to slow time and extend the heating of its contents. Pour the prepared black batter within, and cover it with the pudding. Mix them not!

I received this, as did O. Baer, from Prof. M. Dykes, two days before his disappearance. His letter insisted that I prepare these—the Mounds—at once and place them "in every dreaded corner" of my house.

Scatter all of the dark chocolate morsels over this, and emplace the dome of sealing.

With the flame low, await the signs of setting batter and bubbling essence. When the moment arrives, gouge warm servings from the mass, and top each copiously with the shredded coconut.

The Hounds dwell in the angles of the universe. They may enter our plane where theirs intersects ours — where the appropriate angles appear.

Poor, poor Prof. Dykes. Locked himself inside his study, warning others that "the hounds were on the hunt." Looks like he tried to round off every corner. He has since vanished without a trace. As they say: there is always an angle.

If Time Is Short

You have already transgressed enough to be pursued. If the hunters are nigh, it convicts you no worse to do as instructed with pre-prepared mixes for both prepared elements. All else is the same. When they arrive, place the Mounds before them. They will be unable to resist, affording you precious time to flee again!

What did he discover? What discovered him? It appears that he spent his final hours preparing copious quantities of the Mounds. What did old Dykes get wrong?

My glimpses of the seated hounds were fleeting, blurred. Multiple luminous eyes. Twisting limbs bending the wrong way.

Odd remnants of an unidentifiable substance covering much of the surfaces in Prof. M. Dykes' study. The blue ichor of Tindalos.

The angles — must they be geometric? Angles of time?

The silver candy
        I have
been to the Dreamlands
and seen the sinister black
galleys and the horrid toad-like
rowers. I've seen the looping
courtship ritual of the Shantaks
above lavender cliffs. I have
witnessed the burial rite of the
ghouls in the eternal grey
twilight of the underworld...and
yet I still find it hard to
believe that these metallic orbs
are edible.

Easingham

—It's so familiar.
That horrendous
yellow moss that has
covered the old
town in the Jackson
pines, just as Bäer
had said before
he went missing.

Where did it come from?
Where did it go?

THE CUSTARD OUT OF SPACE

Serves four, to itself

Feff Efments

2 cups milk

1/3 cup sugar

2 tablespoons cornstarch

2 eggs

1 teaspoon vanilla extract

1 banana

4 teaspoons maple syrup

Red and blue food coloring

Sweetworks Sixlets Shimmer Silver candies

Invocation of the Formless One

I seen it. It fell straight inna th' saucepan like a glob of mixed together milk, sugar, an' cornstarch. It were hot, bubblin' at the edges. At first thought I saw clumps, but it span and whirled like it was bein' stirred with a whisk or summat.

It cooled off the heat, and th' bowl next to it had some eggs all beat up . . . an' I swear it slowly drained a bit'o itself into them eggs! Then it all wen' back inna pot, th' heat coming back into it . . . an' slowly risin' all th' time! It thickened like it were just absorbing everything it touched—but it never boiled—like it wouldn't let itself. I know how it sounds!

Next it extracted the vanilla, just stirring and stirring and getting thicker all th' time. Thar were no cooling it off now. I . . . I don't know why, but I picked it up, and I started pouring it into th' good glass bowls. I don't remember cutting up th' banana, but three or four slices went into each bowl. Mind's . . . fuzzy. I think I put in a half teaspoon of syrup in each, with a drop each of the colors. When I were done with all four, I went back and did th' exact same again to make a second layer in each. I don't know why—I'm telling you!

The last thing I remember, was the silver globes rising out of each well. I remember their terrible beauty. Serve the others. Yes. Taste . . .

I have decided that it may be best to remain inside from now on. Nothing has been the same since my last trip to the old house in Jackson. Something came back with me, I'm certain of it. Something from the pines

THE CAKE IN YELLOW

 Serves a small but intimate party of one dozen and four

The Call

1½ cups powdered sugar

1 cup cake flour

1 dozen egg whites at ambient temperature

1½ teaspoons cream of tartar

1 cup sugar

1½ teaspoons vanilla extract

½ teaspoon almond extract

Yellow food coloring

¼ teaspoon salt

Dipping and dressing
preparations of chocolate,
raspberry, lemon, and caramel

*The spirals
for 17 days
3 hours, 24 min*

Each becomes 3

The Revel

Tonight the oven rack reaches its nadir. Aldebaran and Hyades have reached a combined 375 degrees F, and the time is right.

I will mix them like powdered sugar and flour. Separately, unbeknownst to the others, shall I whisk them about like egg whites and cream of the tartar until they are as foam on the shore of Hali!

It is at that point that the wind of sweet sugar shall blow at them, just a bit at a time. I add the extracts, a few drops of the coloring, and salt! Finally, with salt to their wounds, I shall beat them until they are stiff and glossy, like a meringue.

But even then, I am not done. Together shall the separate meet . . . slowly shall they be introduced. Into another shall they disappear and then pushed into an angelic pan measuring shall they go. With patience, and a metallic spatula, press the breath from them! Gently they will be cloven, as with a knife through batter.

Combine and cut thus, shall they revel and bake for one half hour. Dry and pert under my finger shall they be before respite. Immediately, I hang inverted this creation unto a flame-proof surface. Oh, the joy of their cries, as for a pair of hours they hang!

With the long jagged knife, I cut them free . . . and into the shapes of my desire. Coldly then, I consign them, all warmth gone from my voice. They shall bask in my various pleasures until all have been consumed. The show must go on, after all, and others are calling.

I have gathered all the ingredients. Every one.

Message from Durkin, found in my satchel: "Agony's what it is." "He's in agony" one written on each wing of a folded 3-headed crane.

The great Citadel of Carcosa

The pleasing ornateness of the pan is an absolute requirement! Plainness is forbidden!

It is a simple thing: unadorned with the grotesqueries I have come to expect.

d'Ys

Lemon

Raspberry

Caramel

Chocolate

"...Her slender figure was exquisitely set off in the homespun hunting-gown edged with silver, and on her gauntlet-covered wrist she bore one of her petted hawks."

It is necessary to slice the offering into shapes the world most please, lest you toss its entirety to the lowly horde who would tear it to chunks with their hands.

The shapes are just wrong — there is a right way to do this I am certain! To subdivide the imperfect into the perfect.

I haven't touched this book in months, I was sure of it.

I should not have attempted this alone — Many days to make them all.

THE RING THAT SHOULD NOT BE

 Embraces The Coven of Twelve

Forbidden Fragments

1 (15-ounce) can of pear halves, reserve the ichor

4 packets unflavored gelatin

2 (6-ounce) boxes lime gelatin

1 (8-ounce) brick cream cheese

1 teaspoon citric acid

Yellow food coloring

3 tablespoons white sugar

Green food coloring

1 bunch rice noodles

Green sparkle gel icing
  and luster dust of gold and silver

The Relics Thou Needst

Pliable bottle

Tentacle mold

Ring mold

Every window shuttered. I do not hear the knocking. That is not the voice of O. Boer outside

It is the voice from the pines

To Bring Forth the Reaching Arms of Nyogtha

The arms of Nyogtha must be summoned in pears. Break the seal on their prison, and drain forth their juices. Place the halves aside for later use.

In measure should thee have one and one-half chalices of the pears' ichor. Add such boiling water as is needed to make two chalices of liquid, and divide in half.

Place thee one chalice-measure in a small vessel, and rain down upon this two portions of the unflavored gelatin. Allow this to bloom for perhaps one-sixth of an hour, and then stir in three chalices of boiling water, and both portions of the Emerald Gel of Tin. Let Dissolution reign!

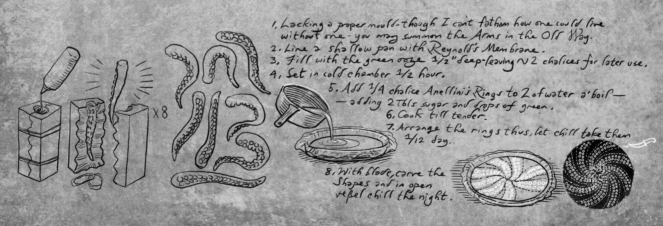

1. Lacking a proper mould—though I can't fathom how one could live without one—you may summon the Arms in the Old Way.
2. Line a shallow pan with Reynold's Membrane.
3. Fill with the green ooze 1/2" deep—leaving ~2 chalices for later use.
4. Set in cold chamber 1/2 hour.
5. Add 1/4 chalice Anellini's Rings to 2 of water a'boil—adding 2 Tbls sugar and drops of green.
6. Cook till tender.
7. Arrange the rings thus, let chill take them 1/12 day.
8. With blade, carve the Shapes and in open vessel chill the night.

In a small cauldron with the flame banked low, pour the preceding mixture. Lower into this the white bar of creamed cheese. Swirl and stir amid the proper incantations until all is one, and the ichor is now a thick and creamy spectral hue. This you will consign to a pliable bottle, narrow at one end, and fill the tentacle mold, that the proper form may be taken! For one-quarter hour this is set in the Chamber of Ice, and thence for one-third hour the greater Hyperborean cavity.

Release the grasping arm, and place this in a vessel open to the chill air of the cavity. Repeat this until eight arms are had to hold thee—saving the remainder.

Rest these through the dark hours in their vessel in Hyperborean air.

Now take up the final chalice of the pear liquid. Pour that which is within into the cauldron, and with patience add the remainder of the unflavored gelatin. This thee shall let bloom one-sixth hour. When the bloom can be seen clearly and the spirit of Nyogtha has taken hold, pour then a double chalice of boiling water, the acid, and the yellow staining solution—enough for the unearthly golden hue to ignite. . . . Form again the Vortex of Dissolution!

This now shall thee pour into the ring. Concern thee naught that it seem not to fill the vessel. Carry the Ring into the refrigerated cavity in the space you have prepared. It will take some hours to firm, perhaps two to four; have patience and continue the ritual labors.

Remelt the green gelatin. This may be done over low heat, or by use of the Casket of Minor Waves. As the ichor melts, crush to paste the cloven pears then combine them with the ichor.

Ready a non-euclidean vessel whose circumference approximates the center of thy ringed form. Pour the hot ichor within, and allow it to cool. Now canst thou form the underlayer for the golden ring.

As with the dead of Egypt, lay these labors in a chill tomb, and allow Set to take them.

Do not flag, do not cease your labors. Thou must boil one chalice of water with one measure of the white sugar mingled with the emerald staining essence. Thence add thee the tendrils from the Far East. Remove and drain them when they are tender, and green of hue.

Complete the Ritual!

Fill a basin with scalding water, in which to submerse briefly the ring. When it has just begun to melt at its edges, invert the ring and allow the grip of the Earth to free it!

Place a seething mass of the tendrils in the center of the ring, and arrange the tentacles radially around the edge.

Free now the emerald ring and place this atop the writhing tentacles.

Anoint the upper reaches of the ring with the green sparkle gel frosting. Dust lightly with silver the tentacles, and with gold the peared body of the ring.

Serve fresh from the chill reaches of the space between spaces! The worthy shall consume and be one, the unworthy shall be consumed and be one! Drain them of their sanity, as they taste the Ring That Should Not Be!

the task is nearly complete

y.
g.
I must work fast as the storm grows fiercer and fiercer. I shall stay here. I shall stay in this room.

They want to be found.

The recipes are coming from the book itself

I saw it

Dear Heaven it

sees me

it sees

me

from the sky

in the sea

into the sky from the sea

APPENDIX: THE RITES REVEALED

— DRINKS —

MARTINI: SHAKEN, NOT HASTUR

The Martini in Yellow
Serves 1

Ingredients

1 squiggle of Kikkoman Wasabi Sauce
4 ounces vodka (preferably Reyka)
4 ounces dry vermouth
1 Spanish olive

Preparation

Place one swirl of wasabi sauce around the rim of the glass (do not complete the circle). Add the vodka and vermouth to a mixing glass and fill with ice.

Shake, and strain into a chilled cocktail glass.

Garnish with a small Spanish olive without pimento for that mindless cosmic horror look.

AT THE FOUNTAINS OF MADNESS

Ooch Look Bears (Italian Sodas)

Serves 1

Ingredients

3 to 6 gummy bears, frozen in ice cubes

10 ounces black cherry seltzer

2 ounces maraschino cherry syrup

1 ounce half-and-half

Additional gummy bears or blobs

Preparation

Freeze the bears into ice cubes within an ice cube tray. Use these bear cubes as the ice for the drinks.

Mix the wet ingredients, add or subtract amounts of the liquids to taste.

Add extra bears to the drink at serving, allow guest to eat or drown the careless victims.

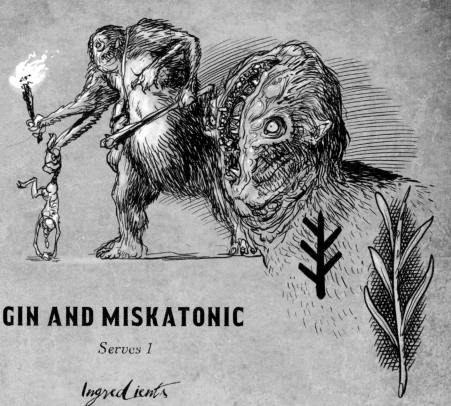

GIN AND MISKATONIC

Serves 1

Ingredients

3 ounces Hendrick's gin

3 lime wedges

4 to 5 ounces tonic water (such as Fever Tree)

1 ounce Hpnotiq liqueur

1 rosemary sprig, trimmed properly, or a twist of lemon peel

Preparation

Add gin to a highball glass filled with ice.

Gently squeeze in the lime wedges to taste, later arrange them in
a triskelion at the edges of the glass.

Add the tonic water; stir to combine.

Pour Hpnotiq over back of spoon to layer on top.

Place cut rosemary sprig prominently in front of glass for protection, or skip if
you're feeling reckless. Can replace with a twist of lemon peel, if preferred.

NOG-SOTHOTH: THE LIQUOR AT THE PUNCH BOWL

Egg Nog
Serves 7

Ingredients

4 egg yolks

⅓ cup plus 1 tablespoon sugar

1 pint whole milk

1 cup heavy cream

1 teaspoon freshly grated nutmeg

4 to 8 ounces Kraken Black Spiced Rum

4 egg whites

1 cup black bubble tea boba tapioca pearls

½ cup light Karo or sugar syrup

Preparation

With a mixer, beat the egg yolks in a large bowl until light and frothy. Add the ⅓ cup sugar gradually, until completely dissolved.

Stir in the milk, cream, nutmeg, and rum.

Separately beat the egg whites to soft peaks in a mixer, then while the mixer is still running add the 1 tablespoon of sugar and beat until stiff peaks form. Chill for one hour.

Whisk the egg whites into the mixture. Divide between the seven glasses, add the tapioca pearls as described below, and serve.

Adding Something to Your Nog:
Preparing the Black Bubble Tea Boba Tapioca Pearls

Add the tapioca pearls to boiling water in a medium saucepan and boil until pearls float—stir to keep them from sticking together. Reduce the heat to medium-high and cook uncovered for 10 minutes, stirring occasionally. Remove the pot from the heat and let stand for 15 minutes. Drain and rinse pearls, transferring to a small container. Add the light syrup to cover the pearls. Spoon into drinks. Yes, between the Kraken and the boba pearls—it's supposed to look like that.

Cook's Note: For cooked eggnog, follow procedure below.

With a mixer, beat the egg yolks until light and frothy. Add the ⅓ cup sugar gradually until completely dissolved. Set aside.

In a medium size saucepan over medium-high heat, add the milk, heavy cream and nutmeg and, stirring occasionally, bring to a boil. Remove from heat and gradually add the hot mixture into the egg and sugar mixture. Then return everything to the saucepan and heat the mixture up to 160 degrees F. Remove from the heat and stir in the rum. Transfer the Nog to a bowl and place in the refrigerator to chill for one hour.

Separately beat the egg whites to soft peaks in a mixer, then while the mixer is still running, add the 1 tablespoon of sugar and beat until stiff peaks form.

Whisk the egg whites into the mixture. Chill and serve.

HERBERT WEST'S DEANIMATOR

A Bright Green Sedative

Serves 1

Ingredients

2 ounces Limoncello Santoni

½ ounce St-Germain elderflower liqueur

1 dash blue curaçtao

2 ounces VDKA 6100

Preparation

Pour the Limoncello into a mixing glass and add the St-Germain and the blue curaçtao.
(Be sure not to add more than a quarter ounce of curaçtao or you'll ruin the radioactive green
colors. It is an important ingredient, but too much will overpower the other flavors.)

Add the VDKA 6100.

Stir thoroughly to integrate. Distribute via test tubes, syringes, or flasks . . .

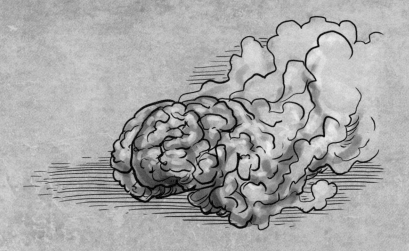

MI-GO BRAIN CYLINDER

Serves 1

Ingredients

1 ounce butterscotch schnapps

1 tablespoon chilled Bailey's Irish Cream

1 drop Red Ice 101 Cool Cinnamon Schnapps Liquor

Preparation

Pour the schnapps into a tall shot glass and slowly pour the
Bailey's into the shot over the back of a tablespoon.

Using an eyedropper, drop (not place, drop!) one drop of
the Red Ice 101 into the center of the glass.

Serve immediately or store in the refrigerator.

SUNKEN MOO

Marinated Steak

Serves 4

Ingredients

1 cup fresh parsley

1 teaspoon dried oregano

3 tablespoons fresh lemon juice

2 large garlic cloves, keep 1 whole and 1 minced

$\frac{1}{4}$ cup plus 5 tablespoons extra virgin olive oil

$\frac{1}{4}$ cup water

1$\frac{1}{2}$ pounds sirloin steak, cubed into 1-inch pieces

1 teaspoon salt, plus more for seasoning

1 teaspoon black pepper, plus more for seasoning

30 cherry tomatoes

2 cups shredded kale

Preparation

Put the parsley, oregano, lemon juice, 1 garlic clove, $\frac{1}{4}$ cup of the olive oil, and water in a blender. Blend until you have a smooth, green sauce.

Remove $\frac{1}{4}$ cup of the sauce and put this into a sealed gallon-size plastic bag with the cubed steak and salt and pepper.

Coat the steak and marinate in the bag, then refrigerate for a minimum of 30 minutes.

Preheat the oven to 375°F.

Move the remaining sauce into a small serving bowl for dipping.

Toss the tomatoes whole with 2 teaspoons of the olive oil.

Season with salt and freshly cracked black pepper.

Put tomatoes onto a foil-wrapped cookie sheet and place into the preheated oven and roast until tomatoes are starting to burst. Don't burn the tomatoes.

Heat a small skillet to medium-high; add 1 tablespoon of oil.

Add in the shredded kale and minced garlic; sauté for 2 to 5 minutes until wilted, dark, and stringy. Season with salt and pepper.

Cook the marinated steak chunks in a large nonstick skillet with 1 tablespoon olive oil over medium-high heat (3 to 4 minutes for medium-rare to medium meat). Evenly brown the steak on both sides.

Remove the steak as they're done and place them on a serving dish.

Skewer tomato and a bit of kale through the steak with a kabob.

THE GRAPE OLD WONS

Baked Beef & Sausage Wontons

Serves 4 (4 appetizers per person)

Ingredients

16 wonton wrappers

$\frac{1}{4}$ pound bulk Italian sausage

$\frac{1}{4}$ pound ground beef

$1\frac{1}{2}$ cups (6 ounces) shredded Colby-Jack cheese

$\frac{1}{2}$ cup mayonnaise (such as Hellman's)

$\frac{1}{4}$ cup sour cream

$\frac{1}{4}$ cup whole milk

2 teaspoons ranch salad dressing (such as Hidden Valley)

16 large firm black or red grapes, peeled and pipped

1 ounce wasabi paste

Sriracha

Preparation

Preheat the oven to 375°F.

Press the wonton wrappers into the cups of a muffin tin—shape to look like petals or open eyelids.

Bake wontons in the preheated oven for 3 minutes or until lightly browned but still pliable.

In a large skillet, cook the sausage and beef together over medium heat until
no longer pink, about 7 minutes. Drain.

In a large bowl, combine the meat mixture, cheese, mayonnaise, sour cream, milk, and salad dressing.

Carefully spoon 2 tablespoons of the mixture into each wonton cup.
Bake for 7 to 8 minutes or until heated through.

Peel or cut off tip of grapes and top (or dot the eye) with wasabi paste.

Press a grape into each cup so the grape eye looks out.

Garnish with Sriracha to make the look of an eye.

Serve warm.

Refrigerate leftovers.

SACRIFICIAL LAMB

Grilled Lamb Fillets

The cabal's notes: slivers of delicately prepared lamb strips on a bed of bean sprouts served with a HUGE knife. Also known as "what to do with the body if the sacrifice goes wrong."

Serves 4

Ingredients

1½ pounds deboned lamb fillets, skinned and cut into thin slices

1 cup roughly chopped parsley

1 cup roughly chopped cilantro

1 cup roughly chopped mint

1 teaspoon ground ginger

2 garlic cloves, crushed

1 teaspoon paprika

½ teaspoon cinnamon

Honey for drizzling and dipping

Salt

Cracked black pepper

2 bunches bean sprouts

Preparation

Put the strips of lamb into a medium glass bowl and add all the ingredients except the honey, salt, pepper, and bean sprouts.

Toss the lamb well so that the strips are well coated with the spices. Set aside and further marinate for 30 minutes.

Thread the lamb onto metal or wooden skewers and season with salt and pepper.

Grill the lamb skewers until brown on one side, flip and cook for an additional minute.

Brush with honey, season with the salt and pepper, and seal on the heat for a few seconds before serving.

Serve on a bed of bean sprouts with a dish of honey for dipping.

ATLACH-NACHOS

Staring Nachos with Legs

Serves 8

Ingredients

½ pound cooked shredded brisket or pulled pork or chicken

Taco seasoning to taste

10 to 12 ounces salsa

10 to 12 ounces guacamole

10 to 12 ounces sour cream

36 tortilla cups or flat round tortilla chips

20 thinly sliced mild Cheddar slices

1 (8-ounce) bag shredded fiesta cheese mix

40 black olives, sliced

30 jalapeños slices

Preparation

Sprinkle the prepared, cooked meat with taco seasoning.

Separate the brisket into 36 1-by-3-inch bundles, and set aside.

Combine the salsa, guacamole, and sour cream in a large bowl—mix together but not too thoroughly. The colors should stay swirled.

Set up 36 tortilla cups, put one teaspoon each of salsa mixture in each.

Cut each meat bundle in half and place in each shell to make an X-shape; cover with a slice of cheese slightly larger than the cup itself.

Bake until the cheese melts to the edge of the cup, sealing in the contents.

Allow to cool, then flip each over.

Scatter some fiesta cheese on the top of the cup.

Place two olive rings for eyes, and a jalapeño on the "back," on top of the cheese.

Bake for another 2 minutes or until melted and the "spider" is complete.

NEW ENGLAND DAMNED CHOWDER

It Gets Me!

Serves 5

Ingredients

5 center-cut bacon strips, thick cut

1 small onion, finely diced

2 stalks celery, chopped

2 small garlic cloves, sliced or mashed

4 potatoes, cubed

1 cup water

1 (8-ounce) bottle clam juice

4 teaspoons chicken bouillon

$\frac{1}{2}$ teaspoon white pepper

$\frac{1}{2}$ teaspoon thyme

$\frac{1}{4}$ cup all-purpose flour

$2\frac{1}{2}$ cups heavy cream

2 (51-ounce) cans chopped clams

1 bunch scallions, diced, for garnish

Preparation

In a dutch oven, cook the bacon over medium heat until crisp. Remove to paper towels to drain.

Sauté the onion, celery, and garlic in the bacon drippings until tender, about 5 minutes.

Stir in the potatoes, water, clam juice, boullion, pepper, and thyme. Bring to a boil.

Reduce heat; simmer, uncovered, for 15 to 20 minutes or until the potatoes are tender.

In a small bowl, combine the flour and $1\frac{1}{2}$ cups of the heavy cream until smooth. Gradually stir into the chowder. Bring to a boil; cook and stir for 1 to 2 minutes or until thickened.

Stir in the clams and remaining heavy cream; heat through (do not boil).

Crumble in the reserved bacon as well as sprinkle bacon on top upon serving, along with the scallions.

PALLID BISQUE

Crab and Shrimp Seafood Bisque

Serves 4 to 6

Ingredients

3 tablespoons unsalted butter

2 tablespoons chopped green onion

2 tablespoons chopped celery

$2\frac{1}{2}$ cups milk

3 tablespoons all-purpose flour

$\frac{1}{2}$ teaspoon freshly ground black pepper

1 tablespoon tomato paste

1 cup heavy whipping cream

8 ounces crab meat

4 to 8 ounces small cooked shrimp or other seafood

4 tablespoons sherry

$\frac{1}{4}$ teaspoon salt

4 to 6 dollops sour cream (1 per serving)

1 cup sticky rice

Preparation

Melt the butter in a large saucepan over medium-low heat; add the chopped green onion and celery.
Sauté and keep stirring until tender.

Warm the milk in another medium saucepan over medium heat.

Blend the flour into the butter and vegetables, for about 2 to 3 minutes.
Slowly stir in the warmed milk and continue cooking and stirring until thickened.
Add the black pepper, tomato paste, and heavy cream.

For a thinner, smoother soup, puree the soup in a blender and then return it to the saucepan.

Stir in the crab, shrimp, and the sherry. Bring to a simmer. Add salt to taste.

Divide the bisque between four serving bowls

Prepare four small patties using the sticky rice, prepared and separated into four equal portions.

Form rice into faces. Place masks onto the soup surface.
Top with a dollop of sour cream on each.

Serve hot.

Feel free to add small cooked bay scallops or
lobster instead of the crab or included with the crab.

INVESTIGATOR GUMBO

Crab, Seafood, and Vegetable Gumbo

Serves 8

Ingredients

1 cup vegetable oil

1 cup all-purpose flour

1 cup chopped onions

1 cup chopped green bell pepper

1 cup chopped red bell pepper

1 cup chopped celery

3 tablespoons minced garlic

3 cups chopped okra

1½ cups amber or lager beer

6 cups seafood or chicken stock

2 bay leaves

2 teaspoons Cajun or "Old Bay" seasoning

1 tablespoons apple cider vinegar

2 tablespoons kosher salt

1½ teaspoons cayenne pepper

1 pound medium fresh shrimp or crawfish, peeled, beheaded, and deveined

1 pound red snapper fillets or white fish, chopped

2 cups shucked oysters

1 cup jumbo lump blue or blue point crab meat, picked free of shells

½ pound alligator meat

¼ cup chopped fresh parsley

2 tablespoons filé powder

Hot cooked rice for 8

Chopped green onion, for garnish (optional)

The Cthuken
is a lie—

Preparation

In an 8-quart stockpot, heat oil over medium heat for about 5 minutes;
add flour, and stir together to form a roux. Cook, stirring often (do not burn)
until roux is the color of peanut butter, about 15 to 20 minutes.

Add the onion, bell peppers, celery, garlic, and okra.
Cook the vegetables, stirring often, for 5 minutes.

Add the beer, stock, bay leaves, Cajun seasoning, vinegar, salt, and cayenne.
Bring mixture to a boil; reduce heat to medium and simmer for about 1 hour.

Add the shrimp, fish, oysters, lump crab meat, and alligator to mixture.
Cook for 8 to 10 minutes or until seafood is cooked through; add the parsley.

Add the filé powder to mixture just before serving. Mix thoroughly.

Serve with rice, and garnish with green onion, if desired.

DINING TRAPEZOHEDRON
Iceberg Lettuce Wedge Salad
Serves 4

Ingredients

2 small tomatoes, diced

Kosher salt to taste

4 to 6 slices of bacon

½ cup fresh bread crumbs

Freshly ground black pepper

4 tablespoons brown sugar

1 large head iceberg lettuce

1 small red onion, minced

Blue Cheese Dressing

(May be substituted with your favorite blue cheese dressing)

2 ounces sharp blue cheese

½ cup mayonnaise

½ cup sour cream

½ cup whole milk

1 tablespoon lemon juice

Freshly ground black pepper

Preparation

Set a mesh strainer over a bowl and add diced tomatoes.
Sprinkle liberally with salt, and toss evenly.

In a small skillet, cook bacon over medium-high heat, until crisped,
not dark or burnt, about 5 minutes. Transfer to a paper towel–lined plate.

Using the rendered bacon fat still in the skillet, add the bread crumbs
and cook over medium heat for 5 to 8 minutes, until browned and crisp.
Transfer to a new paper towel–lined plate to drain; season with salt and pepper.

In a small skillet over low heat, add the finely chopped cooked bacon and stir
occasionally for 5 to 8 minutes. Bacon should be super crisp and deep brown.
Remove the bits and transfer them to another paper towel–lined plate to drain.

Clean out the skillet and reheat on medium low. Add the bacon and brown sugar;
stirring to coat the bacon. Sugar will start to caramelize; watch it closely so it doesn't burn.
Remove from heat when the sugar is dissolved and bacon is coated; cool.

Prepare the dressing: In a medium bowl, whisk the blue cheese, mayonnaise, sour cream, milk,
and lemon juice until a smooth, lumpy cheese dressing forms. Add pepper to taste.

Remove and discard the outer leaves of the lettuce head.
Quarter through the core so that each quarter still holds together.
Arrange iceberg wedges on plates and spoon dressing on each.
Sprinkle onion all over the salad islands, along with tomatoes,
caramelized bacon, and toasted bread crumbs. Serve.

TSATHOGGUAMBALAJA
Seafood Jambalaya with Shrimp and Andouille Sausage
Serves 4 to 6

Ingredients

3 tablespoons olive oil

½ medium onion, chopped

½ green bell pepper, chopped

1 stalk celery, chopped

½ pound andouille sausage, sliced into ¼-inch slices

3 cups cooked rice

1 teaspoon paprika

1 teaspoon black pepper

1 teaspoon dried oregano

½ teaspoon onion powder

½ teaspoon dried thyme

¼ teaspoon garlic salt

1 bay leaf

2 cups chicken broth

1 cup water

1 tablespoon tomato paste

½ teaspoon hot pepper sauce

1 (28-ounce) can diced tomatoes, undrained

½ pound shrimp, peeled and deveined

¼ pound fresh cooked tuna (or freshwater fish of your choice), flaked to 1-inch chunks

¼ pound clams, mussels, or scallops, cooked

2 tablespoons chopped fresh parsley

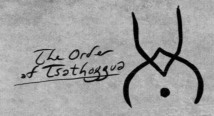

The Order of Tsathoggua

Preparation

Heat olive oil in a large Dutch oven over medium-high heat. Add the onion, bell pepper, celery, and sausage; sauté 5 to 10 minutes or until vegetables are tender.

Add the rice, paprika, black pepper, oregano, onion powder, thyme, garlic salt, and bay leaf.

Cook for 2 minutes.

Add the broth, water, tomato paste, hot pepper sauce, and diced tomatoes; bring to a boil. Cover, reduce heat, and simmer for 20 to 25 minutes.

Add the shrimp, tuna, and clams; continue to simmer for another 5 minutes.

Let stand for 5 minutes. Remove the bay leaf. Stir in the parsley.

AHIÄ! AHIÄ! FATHER DAGON!

Tuna Tartar

Serves 4

Ingredients

3¾ pounds very fresh tuna steak

1¼ cups olive oil

Zest of 5 limes

1 cup freshly squeezed lime juice

2½ tablespoons soy sauce

2 tablespoons hot red pepper sauce (such as Tabasco; optional)

2½ tablespoons kosher salt

1½ tablespoons freshly ground black pepper

1 cup minced scallions, whites and greens

3¼ tablespoons minced fresh jalapeño pepper, seeds removed (optional)

5 ripe Hass avocados

1½ tablespoons toasted sesame seeds

Cooked rice or quinoa, for serving

4 fresh pineapple rings

Preparation

Cut the tuna into ¼-inch dice and place in a very large bowl.

In a separate bowl, combine the olive oil, lime zest, lime juice, soy sauce, hot red pepper sauce, if using, salt, and pepper. Pour over the tuna, add the scallions and jalapeño, if using, and mix well.

Cut the avocados in half, remove the seed, and peel. Cut the avocados into ¼-inch dice. Mix the avocado into the tuna mixture.

Add the sesame seeds and season to taste. Allow the mixture to sit in the refrigerator for at least 1 hour for the flavors to blend.

Form into 2½-inch spheres and serve on a bed of rice or quinoa.

Top each with a pineapple ring.

DEEP-FRIED DEEP ONE

Crab Cakes
Serves 4

Ingredients

1 large egg

1 tablespoon mayonnaise, best quality

1 teaspoon Old Bay seasoning

$\frac{1}{4}$ teaspoon salt

1 teaspoon finely chopped fresh parsley

1 pound lump crab meat (see Note below)

$\frac{1}{2}$ pound fresh salmon

$1\frac{1}{2}$ tablespoons unseasoned bread crumbs, more if needed

3 tablespoons unsalted butter, for cooking

Lemon wedges, for serving

Note: Pick through the crabmeat to remove any remaining pieces of shell or hard and sharp cartilage.

Preparation

Line a baking sheet with aluminum foil.

Combine the egg, mayonnaise, Old Bay, salt, and parsley in a large bowl and mix well.

Add the crabmeat, salmon, and bread crumbs; gently fold mixture together until just combined, being careful not to shred or flatten the meat excessively.

Shape into eight disks (about $\frac{1}{2}$ cup each, up to 1 inch thick) and place on the prepared baking sheet.

Cover and refrigerate for at least 1 hour so they hold their shape when frying.

Heat the butter in a large nonstick pan or skillet, then fry the cakes for about 4 minutes each side or until a brown crust forms on both sides of the crab cake.

Do not move cakes around too much or they will break apart. Be careful of splattering.

Serve with lemon wedges.

THE FISHES FROM OUTSIDE
Roasted Red Snapper and Mixed Garden Peppers
Serves 4

Ingredients

2 large whole snapper fish, cleaned and gutted

15 large garlic cloves, minced

Pinch of salt, plus more to taste

2 teaspoons ground cumin

2 teaspoon ground coriander

1 teaspoon black pepper

1 teaspoon ground sumac

$\frac{1}{2}$ cup chopped fresh dill

4 bell peppers, different colors, sliced in rounds

2 large tomatoes, sliced into rounds

2 medium red onions, sliced into rounds

Olive oil, for the pan and for drizzling

2 lemons

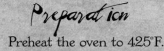

Preparation

Preheat the oven to 425°F.

Pat the snapper fish dry. With a large knife, make two slits on each side of the fish.

Combine the minced garlic with the salt.
Fill the slits and coat the gut cavity of each fish with this mix.

To make the spice mix, combine the cumin,
coriander, salt, pepper, and sumac in a small bowl.

Use three-quarters of the spice mix to season the snapper on both sides;
pat the spices into the fish pushing into the slits you made earlier.
Keep the remainder one-quarter of the spice mix aside for now.

Stuff each gut cavity with the chopped dill, and as much of the sliced peppers,
tomatoes, and onions as possible. Place the stuffed fish on a lightly oiled baking sheet.

Add the remaining sliced vegetables to surround the fish.
Sprinkle the vegetables with a pinch of salt and the remaining spice mix.

Drizzle everything generously with olive oil. Place the baking sheet
on the lower rack of the oven. Roast for 25 minutes until the fish flakes.

Transfer the fish to a serving platter and squeeze juice of one lemon all over it.
Use the slits you made earlier to cut through and portion the fish.

Serve it with wedges of the remaining lemon.

FORMLESS SPAWNGHETTI

Squid Ink Pasta with Shrimp

Serves 3 (4 each)

Ingredients

½ pound squid ink pasta

4 tablespoons lemon juice

2 tablespoons olive oil

2 garlic cloves, chopped

2 tablespoons capers

2 cups chicken broth

½ teaspoon oregano

½ teaspoon parsley

1 teaspoon rosemary salt

5 tablespoons unsalted butter

1 pound shrimp, peeled and deveined

3 (10.5-ounce) packages breadstick dough

1 cup halved cherry tomatoes

Preparation

Preheat the oven to 375°F.

Cook the pasta according to package directions. Drain, rinse, and place in a large bowl. Set aside.

In a separate pan, heat the oil and sauté the garlic and capers for 3 minutes.

Add the chicken broth, oregano, parsley, and salt and bring to a boil. Add the butter then simmer to thicken. Add the shrimp and coat them well, turning them as they simmer.

While reducing the butter sauce, shape the breadstick dough into twelve wells of a muffin tin to form little bread bowls.

Mix the pasta with the lemon butter sauce and shrimp.

Fill the little bread bowls with the pasta and shrimp; use tongs to drape the pasta and create "arms" for the creatures.

Add halved cherry tomatoes as embellishments.

TO CALL FORTH THE SANDWICH HORROR

The Terror between Two Buns

Makes 1 sandwich

Ingredients

1 round pretzel bread roll

1 whole olive, stuffed with goat cheese

1 pound rare roast beef, deli-sliced thin

3 to 5 pickle spears, skinned

1 roasted red pepper

1 cup whole almond shards

1 slice Swiss Cheese, deli-sliced thin, torn roughly round

Pesto sauce, for drizzling

Preparation

Cut out the center of the star shape on the top of the pretzel bun; insert an olive in the cut.

Pile the roast beef on the bottom bun. Position the pickle spears on top of the beef, nestled in the meat and extending out of the sandwich onto the plate like tentacles.

On top of this, place the roasted pepper. Position the open portion of the pepper toward the front of the roll. Insert the almond shards strategically as "teeth."

Place the cheese round on top, and place the bottom bun in a microwave or under the broiler to melt the cheese.

Drizzle sandwiches with pesto and place the top of bun on top.

BYAKHEE GYRO

Gyro Sandwich
Serves 6

Gyro

1 medium onion, plus more chopped onion for serving

2 pounds ground lamb

1 tablespoon finely minced garlic

1 tablespoon dried marjoram

1 tablespoon dried ground rosemary

2 teaspoons kosher salt

½ teaspoon freshly ground black pepper

1 clay brick the size of your loaf pan, wrapped in foil

6 pieces of pita bread, for serving

Chopped tomato, for serving

Feta cheese, for serving

Tzatziki Sauce

16 ounces plain yogurt

1 medium cucumber, peeled, seeded, and finely chopped and drained

Pinch of kosher salt

3 cloves garlic, finely minced

1 tablespoon olive oil

2 teaspoons red wine vinegar

6 mint leaves, finely minced

Preparation

Note: Have a food thermometer available.

Process the onion in a food processor and dry the mix in a towel.

In the food processor, add the dried onion, lamb, garlic, marjoram, rosemary, salt, and pepper and thoroughly process into a fine paste.

Preheat the oven to 325°F. Place a foil-covered brick in the oven as well.

Fold the mixture into a loaf pan with no voids at the edges. Place the loaf pan into a water bath and bake for 1 hour or until the internal temperature of the mixture reaches 165°F.

Remove from the oven and drain off any fat. Place the brick wrapped in aluminum foil directly on the surface of the meat and allow to sit for 15 to 20 minutes, until the internal temperature reaches 175°F.

Slice and serve on pita bread with tzatziki sauce, chopped onion, tomatoes, and feta cheese.

For the tzatziki sauce: In a medium mixing bowl, combine the yogurt, cucumber, salt, garlic, olive oil, vinegar, and mint.

MI-GO TO GO

Portobello Steak Sandwich
Serves 4

Ingredients

4 large portobello mushrooms

Extra virgin olive oil, for drizzling

2 pinches of salt

2 pinches of freshly ground black pepper

2 pinches of garlic powder

2 large beefsteak tomatoes

4 slices sharp or smoked Chedddar

2 ciabatta bread rolls, sliced

4 large cashews, boiled or soaked overnight

4 blackberries

1 sprig fresh thyme

1 tablespoon fresh dill

Preparation

Remove stems from the mushrooms and clean the mushrooms.
Drizzle extra virgin olive oil on both sides of the mushroom.

Season both sides of the mushrooms with 1 pinch each of salt, pepper, and garlic powder.
Place the mushrooms in a medium pan over high heat and cook both sides about 5 minutes.

Slice the tomato to the sizes of portobello mushrooms.

Repeat the same coating as the mushrooms: Use extra virgin olive oil to drizzle,
season with a pinch each of salt, pepper, and garlic powder on both sides.

Place a tomato slice on top of each mushroom. Put a lid on top of the pan.
Allow 2 minutes for tomato slices to soften.

Add the Cheddar slices to the top of the tomato. Cover the pan again and
remove from the heat. Wait until the cheese is completely melted.

Remove the mushroom stacks from the pan and place on one stack on each of the ciabatta slices. Add the cashews and blackberries to each, along with the thyme and dill. Finally, drizzle the stacks with the pan drippings and serve immediately.

— Twist their heads off!

Winooski River, near Montpelier, Vt.
West River in Windham County, past Newfane, Vt
Passumpsic River in Glederia County, above Lyndonville, Vt.
— bodies found but no evidence beyond eyewitness testimony for the bodies fell to less than dust, for their matter was not of this world.
Could they have drowned in the Vermont flood waters? I think not.

Abashed the devil stood and felt how awful goodness was

Death is the escape from time.

Why why does the Voice keep changing?

Vermont Pink as Prof. Dykes calls them, though he has never seen one and they cannot be photographed.

They lived and operated deep w/in those Vermont hills. They are still here somewhere.

They speak like a great distant swarm in the howling winds.

Flightless Siberian
MiGo "Abominable Snowman" based on the description in the J. Bellanso journal, 1952

161

WILBUR WHATELEY'S DUNWICH SANDWICH

Crock Pote Puffed Pork

Serves 8

Ingredients

1 (9-pound) bone-in pork shoulder butt roast

1 (12-ounce) bottle honey brown beer
(such as Samuel Adams Cream Stout)

1 cup apple cider vinegar

1½ (18-ounce) bottles Bull's-Eye
Original BBQ Sauce

⅓ cup brown sugar

Garlic powder, to taste

Onion salt, to taste

Dash ground cayenne pepper, to tate

Paprika, to taste

1 (18-ounce) bottle Bull's-Eye Hickory
Smoked BBQ Sauce

8 slices Boston Brown Bread

Bread-and-butter pickles

Preparation

Put the roast in the crock pot with the beer and apple cider vinegar.

Take one bottle of the original BBQ sauce and pour over the roast, making sure that the meat sticking out of the liquid is fully covered. Any extra can go in the liquid so that the rest of the roast gets that flavor.

Slow cook the roast on low for 12 hours. The meat will be falling apart easily.

Fish out the bones as much as you can before the meat is shredded. Shredding will help you double-check that there are no bones left.

Remove the meat to a cutting board and shred.
Save ⅔ cup of the roasting liquid and place in a large bowl.

In the bowl with the roasting liquid, add the brown sugar, garlic powder, onion salt, cayenne pepper, paprika, hickory smoked BBQ sauce, and the remaining ½ bottle of the original sauce. Mix well. Add the shredded pork to the sauce and mix until thoroughly combined.

Put the pork back into the crock pot and warm until ready to serve.

Place a generous portion of pork onto thick-cut slices of the Boston Brown Bread and top with the pickles.

INNSMOUTH SHUCK

Oysters Lovecraft

Serves 2

Ingredients

12 Chesapeake Bay oysters

2 cups spinach

1 cup arugula

2 spring onions

1 garlic clove

3 strips cooked bacon

1 tablespoon unsalted butter

Freshly squeezed lemon juice

2 tablespoons hot sauce

¼ cup grated Gruyère

¼ cup grated Parmesan

Preparation

Heat the oven to 450°F.

Place the shucked oysters on the half shell on a foil-covered baking sheet.

Chop the spinach, arugula, onions, garlic, and bacon. Place them all except the bacon into a skillet.

On medium heat add the butter and sauté until the spinach is wilted.

Add the bacon and drizzle with lemon juice and hot sauce, then stir lightly until heated through.

Place the mixture on the oysters and cover with the cheese. Place in the oven and cook for 10 minutes or until the oysters are warmed through.

SHOGGHOULASH

Beef and Tomato Goulash with Potato Shoggoth Balls

Serves 4

Ingredients

1⅓ pounds ground beef

2 teaspoons salt plus more as needed, to taste

Ground black pepper, to taste

½ cup diced sweet onion

½ cup thin strips green pepper

1 garlic clove, minced

1 (14.5-ounce) can diced tomatoes, drained

8 ounces Italian tomato sauce

3 cups precooked mashed potatoes, chilled

½ cup shredded Cheddar

4 strips bacon, chopped

¼ to ½ cup milk

2 ounces pearl onions

2 ounces cooked black-eyed peas

Paprika for dusting

Cooking spray (such as Pam)

Preparation

For the goulash: In a large skillet over a high heat, cook the ground beef,
salt and pepper to taste, diced onion, and green pepper until ground beef is browned.
Drain and reserve the cooking liquid and set aside.

Reduce to medium heat and add the garlic, drained diced tomatoes,
and tomato sauce until cooked throughout.

Place the mixture on a platter.

For the shoggoth balls: Preheat the oven to 425°F. Mix the precooked mashed potatoes with the
reserved cooking liquid from the beef, along with the Cheddar, bacon, and 2 teaspoons salt.
Form this mixture into four round balls. If balls are lumpy or the balls won't form,
add a bit of milk as necessary until they hold their shape.

Insert the pearl onions and peas, randomly spaced, into the surface of the balls.
Reform to a round shape as necessary.

Place the potato balls onto a greased baking sheet. Lightly dust with paprika to add color
and spray with cooking spray. Bake until golden and warm throughout, about 20 minutes.
Serve on top of the bed of goulash.

ALBINO PENGUIN AU VIN BLANC

Penguin (Chicken) Breast

Serves 4

Ingredients

4 bone-in, skinless Giant Albino Penguin breasts
(chicken breasts are okay)

¼ cup vinegar

½ teaspoon salt, plus more to taste

½ freshly ground black pepper,
plus more to taste

1 cup white wine (dry Riesling or Chardonnay),
more if needed

4 strips bacon, chopped

3 garlic cloves, minced

1 white onion, finely chopped

1 pound portobello mushrooms, sliced

1 cup heavy cream

Chopped parsley, for topping

Cooked rice or pasta, for serving

Preparation

Put the penguin breasts in a large bowl with a mix of vinegar, salt, and pepper,
adding enough white wine to cover completely. Let marinate for 3 days in the fridge,
submerged and covered. If you substituted with chicken breast, skip this step.

Pat dry the breasts with paper towels, season with salt and pepper, and set aside.

Sauté the bacon on medium heat in a large pan for 3 minutes.
Fry the garlic in the rendered fat until golden, about 2 minutes.

Add the onion and portobellos, and cook until the bacon is crispy,
about 6 minutes. Remove everything from the pan and set aside.

Add the breasts to the pan and sear over high heat. Return everything to the pan,
and cook until done, about 3 to 4 minutes, turning the breasts once. Add more white
wine if needed and a pinch of salt. Simmer for 15 to 20 minutes, covered.

Add the cream and a pinch of pepper and simmer for 4 to 5 minutes more.

Plate the breasts and pour the sauce on top. Top with the parsley. Serve with rice or pasta.

CURRIED FAVOR OF THE OLD ONES

Slow Cooker Sweet Potato Chicken Curry

Serves 4

Ingredients

1 teaspoon turmeric powder

½ teaspoon ground coriander

½ teaspoon salt

1 tablespoon sugar

3 tablespoons sweet curry powder

2 pounds chicken breasts

2 (15-ounce) cans coconut milk

2 tablespoons unsalted butter, plus more to grease the slow cooker

2 garlic cloves, crushed

3 sweet potatoes, cut into 1-inch cubes

1 medium sweet onion, cut into 1-inch pieces

3 red beets, pickled, cut into 1-inch cubes

Cooked jasmine rice, for serving

Preparation

In a small bowl, combine the turmeric, coriander, salt, sugar, and sweet curry powder.
Mix thoroughly.

Place the chicken breasts in a buttered 4-to-6-quart slow cooker. Add ¾ cup water and the coconut milk, and make sure to lift up the chicken breasts to prevent the chicken from burning.

Add the butter, garlic, and the bowl of seasoning ingredients. Stir to combine the seasonings.

Add the sweet potatoes, onion, and beets. Stir to combine.

Cover the slow cooker and set to low for 6 to 8 hours, or high for 4 to 6 hours.

Serve with jasmine rice.

THE FATE OF THE ELDER THINGS

Eggplant Parmesan

Serves 4

Ingredients

1 large eggplant

5 large eggs

½ cup all-purpose flour

1 cup extra virgin olive oil

1½ cups of Italian breadcrumbs

1 large jar marinara sauce

1 star fruit

8 ounces mozzarella

4 ounces shredded Cheddar

⅔ cup whole milk

⅓ cup heavy whipping cream

¼ teaspoon garlic powder

¼ teaspoon onion powder

Removing the internals. No need to be clean about it.

Horizontal cuts to assist in removing the meat

Tekeli-li!

Preparation

Clean and remove the top 1 to 2 inches of your eggplant. Set aside the top portion.
Slice vertically between the skin to separate the eggplant from its skin, preserving the
shell—but do not separate the bottom!

Make four vertical cuts, roughly $\frac{1}{4}$ inch wide, through the sides of the shell, starting $\frac{1}{2}$ inch below
the neck, and to within 1 inch or so of the bottom so you may see through it.

Quarter and re-quarter the removed innards of eggplant to bite-sized pieces.

Place these cubes onto paper towel or parchment paper, and sprinkle salt over the pieces.
Let sit for 10 minutes, then pat dry the prepared pieces.

In a large bowl whisk the eggs until frothy. Mix the flour and breadcrumbs in a sizable container.
Dip the eggplant into the egg and then coat with the breadcrumb mix.

Heat the olive oil in a low pan to a medium-high heat and cook the eggplant until they brown.
Set aside on a paper towel.

In a small pan, melt the cheeses on low heat, then stir in the milk and cream, whisking patiently until
smooth, adding the garlic and onion powder.

In another small pan, heat the marinara sauce.

Slice a central slab $\frac{1}{2}$ inch thick from the star fruit, and remove the outside skin from it.

To Serve

Place the preserved eggplant skin upright in the center of a plate. Pour the Marinara sauce around
it. Fill the skin with the hot, melted cheese allowing the cheese to flow out through the cut slits, add
the cubed and breaded eggplant around the skin, and top with the star fruit. Scoop and dip to eat.

FOUL-LAFEL

Fafafel

Serves 4

Ingredients

1 cup dried chickpeas

1 cup roughly chopped onion

2 tablespoons chopped fresh parsley

2 teaspoons salt

1 teaspoon cumin

1 teaspoon dried hot red pepper

4 garlic cloves

1 teaspoon baking powder

4 to 6 tablespoons all-purpose flour

1 package or jar baby corn

Vegetable oil, enough for 3 inches in the pot

4 pieces pita bread

Chopped tomato, for garnish

Diced onion, for garnish

Diced green bell pepper, for garnish

Pickled turnips, for garnish

Tahini sauce, for drizzling

Preparation

Place the chickpeas in a large bowl and add enough cold water to cover them by at least 2 inches. Let them soak overnight and then drain. Or use canned drained chickpeas as a quick substitute.

Place the drained chickpeas and the onion in the bowl of a food processor fitted with a steel blade. Add the parsley, 1 teaspoon of the salt, cumin, hot pepper, and garlic. Process until blended. Don't puree.

Sprinkle in the baking powder and 4 tablespoons of the flour, and pulse. You want to add enough flour so that a dough forms that is not sticky. If the dough is still too wet, add more flour. Turn into a bowl and refrigerate, covered, for a minimum of 2 hours.

In a large pot, boil water and add the baby corn and a teaspoon of salt, cooking for 4 to 6 minutes or until the corn is tender. Set the corn aside on paper towels to dry and cool.

Form the chickpea mixture into $1\frac{1}{2}$-inch balls; it should produce roughly 20 balls.

Heat 3 inches of oil to 375°F in a deep pot, skillet, or wok, and fry one ball to test. If it falls apart, add a little more flour to help keep its shape. Then fry the balls for a few minutes on each side, or until golden brown. Drain on paper towels.

Stuff half a pita with the falafel balls, chopped tomatoes, onion, green pepper, and pickled turnips.

Slice the baby corn lengthwise into 4 wedge-shaped strips and garnish so strips hang halfway out of the bread. Drizzle with tahini sauce.

CTHUS-KOOS

Tuna Couscous

Serves 4

Ingredients

½ package or jar baby corn, sliced carefully and quartered, for garnish

1 teaspoon kosher salt, plus more to taste

1 cup Israeli couscous

4 ounces tuna, drained, and flaked

1 teaspoon lemon zest

¼ cup olive oil

¼ cup pitted, black olives, sliced into rings

1 tablespoon capers, drained

1 cup pesto

¼ cup diced roasted red peppers

1 garlic clove, minced

1 teaspoon freshly ground black pepper

¼ cup freshly squeezed lemon juice

1 cup chopped scallions

Preparation

In a medium pot over high heat, bring water to a boil and add the baby corn and
1 teaspoon salt for 4 to 6 minutes, or until corn is tender and floppy.
Set the baby corn aside on paper towels to dry and cool.

In a medium saucepan over high heat, boil 4 cups of water and add the couscous. Reduce the heat,
cover the pot and simmer for 15 minutes, or until the couscous is just tender. Drain and set aside.

In a large bowl, combine the tuna, lemon zest, olive oil, olives, capers, pesto, red peppers,
garlic, and salt and black pepper to taste. Pour the hot couscous into the mixture and stir well.
Cover and set aside for 10 to 15 minutes, stirring occasionally.

Just before serving, stir in the lemon juice, scallions, and more salt if needed.
Garnish with the strips of baby corn so that strips hang halfway out of the top.

THE UNKNOWN KA'SQUASH

Roasted Spaghetti Squash

Serves 4

Ingredients

1 large spaghetti squash

Salt, to taste

Freshly ground black pepper, to taste

2 tablespoons brown sugar

2 tablespoons extra virgin olive oil

$\frac{1}{4}$ cup finely sliced fresh basil leaves

1 clove garlic, finely chopped

$\frac{1}{4}$ cup grated Parmesan, plus more for topping

2 ripe tomatoes, halved

$\frac{3}{4}$ cup shredded mozzarella

Preparation

Preheat oven to 375°F. Halve the squash and remove the seeds. Place the squash halves onto a high-sided bake pan. Season with salt and pepper to taste. Arrange the spaghetti squash halves cut sides down and pour 1 cup of water evenly into the pan. Bake for about 1 hour, until the squash is baked through and tender. Flip the squash cut sides up and season with brown sugar and let cool until warm. Shred the squash with a fork to create noodles and scrape free from the skins. Drain the noodles to remove excess liquid.

Lightly grease a cookie sheet or bake pans.

In a large mixing bowl, add the squash noodles, olive oil, basil, garlic, a generous amount of salt and pepper, and the Parmesan and coat the noodles evenly. Separate the mixture into 4 piles on the sheet. Press the halved tomatoes into the top of the piles. Sprinkle with mozzarella cheese and a little bit more freshly grated Parmesan. Bake for 30 minutes or until the cheese is bubbly and starting to brown. Serve.

THE SIDE DISH NOT TO BE NAMED

Creamed Spinach with Pearl Onions and Bok Choy
Serves 4

Ingredients

2 tablespoons olive oil

¾ cup pearl onions

¾ cup spinach

⅓ cup bok choy, cut to thin strips

Kosher salt, to taste

Freshly ground black pepper, to taste

Pinch of nutmeg

1 tablespoon all-purpose flour

½ cup milk

¾ cup shredded Colby-Jack

Preparation

Heat 1 tablespoon of the oil in a large skillet over medium-high heat.

Add the onions and cook until the onions are translucent and the edges get browned.
Add the spinach, bok choy, salt and pepper to taste, and nutmeg and cook for 5 minutes or
until spinach is wilted. Remove the skillet from the heat and set aside.

Heat the remaining oil in a large pot over medium heat. Whisk in the flour and cook until bubbling
(about 2 minutes—keep stirring). Add in the milk slowly and continue to whisk until bubbling again.

Remove from the heat. Add the cheese and mix until melted and smooth.

Add the vegetable mixture to the cheese and mix until well combined,
adding additional salt and pepper to taste.

TCHO-TCHO CHOW-CHOW
Roasted Cauliflower with Pepper Relish

Serves 6 (about 6 cups)

Ingredients

1 cauliflower head

2 small yellow onions, diced

1 cup distilled white vinegar

1 cup fresh lemon juice

2 teaspoons kosher salt

$\frac{1}{2}$ cup sugar

$\frac{1}{2}$ teaspoon dried crushed red pepper

2 yellow bell peppers, diced

2 red bell peppers, diced

8 banana peppers, diced

2 tablespoons minced fresh thyme

1 ounce Zayda's horseradish

Preparation

Place the head of cauliflower in a large sauce pan. Add the onions, vinegar, lemon juice, salt, sugar, crushed red pepper, and 1 cup water and bring to a boil. Reduce to simmer, stirring occasionally for about an hour, or until mixture is reduced to about $1\frac{1}{2}$ cups.

Stir in the peppers and cook for 5 minutes, stirring occasionally.
Remove the pot from the heat and let stand for 30 minutes.

Stir in the thyme and horseradish. The cauliflower should be cooked until soft and easy to combine with other ingredients. Serve immediately.

May be refrigerated for up to 3 days, but add fresh thyme and horseradish before serving.

THE MUESLI OF ERICH ZANN

Sounds Delicious

Serves 4

Ingredients

1⅓ cups rolled oats

1 cup milk (whole, coconut, or almond)

1⅓ cups vanilla or plain 4% fat yogurt

4 Granny Smith apples, reserve some for topping

¼ cup sliced almonds, reserve some for topping

½ cup dried strawberries

½ cup dried blueberries

¼ cup sunflower seeds

4 teaspoons honey

Preparation

Soak the rolled oats in milk for 10 minutes.
When the oats have soaked up most of the milk, add in the yogurt.

Shred two of the apples with a cheese grater, and add this to the oats. Slice the other two apples into slivers. Cut the slivers in half. Mix most of this into the oats as well.

Mix in half of the almonds, all of the berries and seeds, and drizzle with the honey. Top with apple slivers and almond slices.

Cover and let chill overnight.

VEGEMITEY CTHULHU

Something about Toads…

Serves 1

Ingredients

2 slices pumpernickel

2 teaspoons unsalted butter

2 tablespoons Vegemite (or Marmite or spicy plum sauce)

2 cups bean sprouts

2 large eggs

Preparation

Make a hole in the center of each piece of bread. You can discard the removed rounds of bread.

Brush a bit of the butter and Vegemite onto each piece (to taste).

In a large skillet over medium heat, melt some of the remaining
butter and place the bread in the skillet.

Scatter half the bean sprouts around the bread, stirring and turning them occasionally.

Carefully break and pour an egg into each hole in the bread. Try to keep the yolk intact.

Maintain medium heat, and after about 2 minutes, turn each piece of bread over.
The egg should have set enough to allow this.

Brush the bread with more butter and Vegemite.

After about another minute, plate and garnish with uncooked bean sprouts.

YOGASH THE GRUEL

This recipe is perfect for long, cold winter mornings but be warned, while it might warm your belly, it may well haunt your soul.

Serves 1

Ingredients

1 cup black rice

Pinch of salt

1 cup whole milk

2 teaspoons sugar

½ teaspoon vanilla extract

Black food coloring

White icing (optional)

Butter, cream, and/or brown sugar for toppings (optional)

Preparation

Start by first rinsing and soaking your black forbidden rice in water overnight. This will make it cook faster and result in a more tender final product.

Prior to cooking, rinse one last time and drain fully.

Place the rice in a large pot with 2 cups water and salt. Bring to a boil and reduce to a simmer. Cover pot with a tight-fitting lid and allow to cook for approximately 20 minutes.

At the 20-minute mark, add in your milk, sugar, and vanilla. Continue cooking uncovered for approximately 20 minutes more, stirring continuously.

At this point, your gruel may be more of a deep purple than black, depending on how thoroughly you rinsed it the night before. Add a few drops of black food coloring to darken the rice to the desired color.

Continue cooking, checking occasionally for doneness. The finished rice should be soft yet slightly chewy.

To serve, spoon into a bowl and drizzle with the icing, if desired. You can also add your choice of toppings, including fresh butter, heavy cream, or brown sugar.

GREAT OLD BUNS

Very Cross Bun

Makes 12 buns

Buns

1 tablespoon active dry yeast

3 cups all-purpose flour

1 tablespoon instant powdered milk

¼ cup sugar

½ teaspoon salt

1 egg

1 egg white

3 tablespoons unsalted butter, softened,
plus more to prepare pans

¾ cup dried cranberries

1 teaspoon cinnamon, plus more for dusting

1 egg yolk

Icing Mix

½ cup confectioners' sugar

¼ teaspoon vanilla extract

2 teaspoons milk

Preparation

Combine ¾ cup warm water, approximately 110°F, and the yeast
in a stand mixer bowl for about 5 minutes.

Add the flour, powdered milk, sugar, salt, egg, and egg white.
Using a dough hook, mix on low speed for 10 minutes.

Add the softened butter, craisins, and cinnamon and mix for an additional 5 minutes.
Transfer the dough to a greased bowl, cover, and allow it to rise until doubled, about 1 hour.

Punch down the dough onto a floured surface, cover, and let rest 10 minutes.
Then divide the dough into twelve balls and place these onto a greased 9-by-12-inch pan.
Cover and let rise in a warm place till doubled, about 40 minutes.

Preheat the over to 375°F

Mix the egg yolk and 2 tablespoons water. Brush onto the buns.

With a sharp knife lightly cut a cross pattern across the top of each bun.
Sprinkle a small amount of cinnamon into each of the cuts.

Bake in the preheated oven for 15 to 20 minutes.

Remove from the pan immediately and cool on a wire rack.

To make the icing: Mix together the confectioners' sugar, vanilla, and milk. Pipe onto the cuts of each bun.

THE OATS OF DAGON

Apple Crumb Squares

Makes 16 squares

Ingredients

2 cups rolled oats

1½ cups all-purpose flour

12 tablespoons (1½ sticks) unsalted butter, melted

1 teaspoon cinnamon

¼ teaspoon salt

½ teaspoon baking soda

¼ teaspoon nutmeg

1 cup light brown sugar, packed

1 cup applesauce

½ cup crushed almonds

6 strips cooked bacon, crumbled

1 teaspoon powdered sugar

Preparation

Preheat the oven to 350°F.

Stir the ingredients (except the applesauce, almonds, bacon, and powedered sugar) in a large mixing bowl until the crumb mixture is evenly moist. Remove 1 cup of the mixture and set aside.

Pour the remaining mix into a greased 9-by-13-inch baking dish and evenly press the mixture into the dish. Bake for 15 minutes so a crust is formed.

Remove the dish from the oven and spread the applesauce and almonds over the crust.

Add the crumbled bacon.

Spread the remaining 1 cup of crumb mixture over top; sprinkle the powdered sugar on top. Bake 12 to 15 minutes and let cool completely (at least 15 minutes).

Cut into squares.

CULTISTS IN ROBES

Pigs in a Blanket

Serves 6 kids

Ingredients

12 breakfast sausages

1 (8-ounce) package biscuit or croissant roll dough

Mustard, ketchup, or barbeque sauce for dipping

Preparation

Preheat the oven to 375°F.

With a sharp, pointed knife, cut from the middle of each sausage vertically through the end. Rotate the sausage and cut again, taking care to leave all portions attached.

You can cut the resulting four sections in half again if you like (lengthwise, to make 8 "legs").

Cut a thin strip of dough. It should be slightly longer than the sausages.

Wrap the dough around the cut sausages, pinching at the uncut side of the sausage to form the cowl, and wrapping the rest, loosely at the bottom where the cuts were made.

Insert two toothpicks into each sausage, forming an X in the middle, just above the cuts. Place each of them upright in muffin pan wells.

Use the knife or another toothpick to splay the "legs" evenly so you can nestle them properly in the wells.

Bake in the preheated oven for 13 minutes. The dough should be a golden brown.

Serve with mustard, ketchup, or barbeque sauce for dipping.

YIGGY PUDDING

Who Combines the Father of Serpents and Chocolate

Pudding . . . WE DO!

Serves 8

Ingredients

1 (3.9-ounce) package chocolate instant pudding

2 cups cold milk

2 ounces chocolate sprinkles

Maraschino cherries, plus more for topping

16 gummy worms

Preparation

Pour the dry pudding mix into a large bowl, then add the cold milk.

Whisk them together until all of the dry pudding dissolves and it's smooth and free of lumps.
Let sit until it thickens, about 5 minutes.

Mix in the sprinkles and maraschino cherries.

Divide the pudding mixture evenly between eight cups.

With a sharp knife, cut slits along the end of the worms so they look menacing with open "mouths."

Insert 2 gummy worms into each pudding cup so a majority of the worms stick out.
Place a few more cherries on top of the serving so they are visible.

Refrigerate before serving.

LOVECRAFT MACARONI AND CHEESE

Serves 6 to 8

Ingredients

2 (7.25-ounce) boxes Kraft Macaroni & Cheese

2 cups milk

2 tablespoons unsalted butter

1 cup shredded mozzarella

2½ cups shredded extra-sharp Cheddar

1 (12-ounce) package spinach fettuccine

1 cup frozen peas

½ teaspoon salt

¼ teaspoon freshly ground black pepper

Preparation

Prepare both boxes of macaroni and cheese as per the instructions, using the milk and butter. Sprinkle with the shredded cheeses when finished.

Prepare the fettuccine as per the instructions, al dente is recommended so that they have some firmness.

Place the frozen peas directly into a small pan of boiling water, and remove them while still bright and firm.

On shallow plates, make a layer of mac and cheese. Scatter a handful of fettuccine over this, followed by a scattering of peas. Then do a second, smaller layer of each.

Season with salt and/or pepper if desired.

SHOGG-POCKETS
Serves 4

Ingredients

1 teaspoon unsalted butter

8 ounces pizza dough

1 cup tomato sauce

½ cup slices of pepperoni, thick and quartered

½ cup meatballs

½ cup shredded mozzarella

½ cup shredded Cheddar

Preparation

Preheat the oven to 375°F. Butter a baking sheet.

Make as many irregular shapes of the dough as will fit,
with room to expand without touching each other.

Leaving room at the edges, coat most of the inside of each with the tomato sauce.

Sprinkle some of the pepperoni on each. Distribute the meatballs toward the center.

Cover with shredded mozzarella and Cheddar.

Place a second layer of pizza dough, roughly the same shape as the bottom pieces, over each.
Pinch or roll the edges together to seal them. Holes, or incomplete coverage, on the top is fine.

Bake in the preheated oven for about 15 minutes, depending on size, thickness, and number.

TO SUMMON NYARLATHOTAPIOCA

Pomegranate Tapioca Pudding
Serves 4

Ingredients

3 cups whole milk

½ cup quick-cooking tapioca beads

½ cup sugar

¼ teaspoon salt

2 eggs, beaten

½ teaspoon vanilla extract

¼ cup pomegranate seeds

¼ cup blackberry jam

12 red grapes, peeled

Preparation

In a medium saucepan over medium heat, mix the milk, tapioca, sugar, and salt. Bring the mixture to a boil, stirring constantly. Reduce the heat to low; cook and stir 5 minutes longer.

Whisk 1 cup of the hot milk mixture into the beaten eggs, 2 tablespoons at a time until incorporated. Stir the egg mixture back into the tapioca until well mixed.

Bring the pudding to a gentle simmer over medium-low heat; cook and stir 2 minutes longer until the pudding becomes thick enough to evenly coat the back of a spoon.

Remove from the heat and stir in the vanilla and pomegranate seeds, and then fold the blackberry jam into the mix (allow some ribbon effects from the jam). Add the peeled grapes.

The pudding may be served hot or poured into serving dishes and refrigerated several hours until cold.

YOGSICLES

Yogurt Ice Pops

Serves 8

Ingredients

8 round ice molds

2½ cups blueberries or blackberries

2 tablespoons agave syrup, more if needed

2 cups 4% fat vanilla yogurt

Preparation

Have the ice molds (or ice cube trays) uncovered and ready.

Blend the blueberries in a food processor or blender on high speed into a chunky to smooth consistency.

Pour the thick liquid into a large bowl. Stir in the agave. Add the yogurt and very gently mix everything together. You want a tie-dye, swirly look to your ice pops; keep visible patches of white and blue. The mixture will be thick. Add more agave for sweetness if needed.

Pour mixture evenly into the bottom half of each mold and tap the mold for the mixture to settle fully, and place the top half carefully on each. Pour the rest of the mix into a plastic bag with one corner removed, and fill the rest of the mold through the top hole. This will give two different textures for each globe. Insert wooden sticks through each hole.

Freeze for 6 hours or overnight. Run warm water over the molds to remove.

MOON-BEAST PIES

Chocolate Whoopee Pies with Strawberry Jam

Serves 12

Pies

8 tablespoons (1 stick) unsalted butter, softened

1 cup sugar

1 egg

1 cup evaporated milk

1 teaspoon vanilla extract

2 cups all-purpose flour

$\frac{1}{2}$ teaspoon salt

$1\frac{1}{2}$ teaspoons baking soda

$\frac{1}{2}$ cup unsweetened cocoa powder

$\frac{1}{2}$ teaspoon baking powder

Marshmallow Filling

8 tablespoons (1 stick) unsalted butter, softened

1 cup confectioners' sugar

$\frac{1}{2}$ teaspoon vanilla extract

1 cup marshmallow crème or fluff

Strawberry Filling

1 (12-ounce) package spaghetti

1 (3-ounce) package strawberry Jell-O

1 cup strawberry jam

Preparation

Preheat the oven to 400°F.

In a large bowl, mix well the butter and sugar,
then mix in the egg, evaporated milk, and vanilla extract.

In a separate medium bowl, mix together the flour, salt, baking soda,
cocoa powder, and baking powder.

Add the flour mixture slowly to the sugar mixture while stirring.
Mix just until all ingredients are combined.

Drop the dough onto a greased cookie sheet by large rounded spoonfuls. Leave at least 3 inches in
between each one; the dough will spread as it bakes.

Bake in the oven for 6 to 8 minutes, until firm when pressed with a finger.
Allow to cool for at least 1 hour before filling.

For the marshmallow filling: In a medium mixing bowl, blend together all
the filling ingredients until smooth.

Break the spaghetti stalks in half and add to a large pot of boiling water. Add the Jell-O
powder to the pot and mix together. Cook until the spaghetti is tender.

Assemble the pies by spreading 2 tablespoonfuls of filling on the flat side of a cookie crust, add
some red spaghetti to stick out from the cookie and a spoonful of strawberry jam onto the filling
just off center, then cover filling with the flat side of another cookie.

Jam should ooze out of one side of pie with the tentacles.

The central feelers of the
Moon-beast are sucked into the head,
bringing the food to an inner, circular
mouth, ringed with round, white crushing
teeth. No dissection has ever been performed,
but when they're dropped from a great height,
their bloated masses burst open.

JOE SLATER'S IN-BREAD PUDDING

New Orlean-Style Bread Pudding with Whiskey Sauce

Serves 12

Whiskey Sauce

8 tablespoons (1 stick) unsalted butter

¼ cup bourbon or other whiskey

1 cup sugar

2 tablespoons water (or more whiskey)

¼ teaspoon freshly grated or ground nutmeg

Dash of salt

1 large egg

Red food coloring

Pudding

3 tablespoons unsalted butter, softened

2 loaves French or Italian bread (about 1¼ pound)

1 cup raisins

2 teaspoons cinnamon

3 large eggs

4 cups whole milk

2 cups sugar

2 tablespoons vanilla extract

Buttercream Icing

1½ cups confectioners' sugar

½ teaspoon vanilla extract

8 tablespoons (1 stick) unsalted butter

1 tablespoon whipping cream

Preparation

For the whiskey sauce: Melt the butter over low heat in a heavy saucepan. Stir in the remaining sauce ingredients, except the egg and food coloring, and blend until the sugar has melted. Remove from heat and whisk until frothy.

Vigorously whisk the egg into the mixture. Set the mixture over medium heat and gently mix until the sauce simmers. Cook until the mix thickens; roughly a minute. The mixture will not curdle.

For the pudding: Preheat the oven to 375°F.

Spread 3 tablespoons butter over a 13-by-9-inch glass baking dish.

Cut the bread into $\frac{1}{2}$-inch slices. Arrange the slices almost upright into tightly spaced rows into the baking pan, adding raisins and light dustings of cinnamon between the slices of bread.

In a large bowl, whisk the three eggs until they are frothy and add the milk, sugar, vanilla, and rest of the cinnamon. Whisk until combined. Pour the mixture over the bread and let it stand for 1 hour. Press the bread down now and again to keep the bread tops wet.

Bake the bread roughly 1 hour until the top is puffed and lightly brown. Cover with three-quarters of the whiskey sauce. Let cool for 30 to 60 minutes.

For the icing: Using a mixer fitted with a whisk, gently mix together the confectioners' sugar, vanilla, and butter. Mix on low speed until well blended and then increase speed to medium and beat further until smooth. Add the cream and continue to beat on medium speed for 1 minute more, adding more cream if needed for spreading consistency.

Spread evenly over the cooled bread..

Mix a few drops of red food coloring into the remaining whiskey sauce.

Pipe decorative patterns into frosting using a straw. Pour the remaining red whiskey sauce over the cut squares of pudding. Serve.

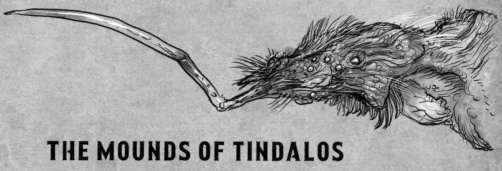

THE MOUNDS OF TINDALOS
Slow Cooker Chocolate Lava Cake

Serves 6 to 8

Chocolate Cake

4 tablespoons (½ stick) unsalted butter, melted

1 cup sugar

1 egg

1 teaspoon vanilla extract

1 cup all-purpose flour

½ cup baking cocoa

1 teaspoon baking soda

1 teaspoon baking powder

2 pinches of salt

Cooking spray

1 (10-ounce) package dark chocolate chips

2 cups shredded sweetened coconut

Pudding

1 cup sugar

½ cup baking cocoa

¼ cup cornstarch

½ teaspoon salt

4 cups milk

2 tablespoons unsalted butter

2 teaspoons vanilla extract

Preparation

For the cake: In a large bowl, cream the butter and sugar until light and fluffy.

Add the egg, beating well. Beat in the vanilla.

In another bowl, whisk the flour, cocoa, baking soda, baking powder, and salt; add to the creamed mixture in parts, beating well after each addition.

Stir in 1 cup hot water until blended.

For the pudding: In a large heavy saucepan, combine the sugar, cocoa, cornstarch, and salt. Gradually add the milk.

Bring to a boil over medium heat; boil and stir for 2 minutes. Remove from the heat; stir in the butter and vanilla.

Spray a 6-quart slow cooker with cooking spray. Pour the prepared chocolate cake mix into the slow cooker.

Pour the prepared pudding mix over the cake batter. Do not mix.

Sprinkle the chocolate chips over top. Cover; cook on low heat for $2\frac{1}{2}$ to 3 hours or until the cake is set and the pudding is beginning to bubble out of the cake.

Spoon the dish to plate and top with shredded coconut. Serve.

In a Hurry Recipe: Follow the previous instructions but use a prepared chocolate cake box mix as well as a prepared box pudding mix, with chocolate chips. It is then cooked and served same as above.

THE CUSTARD OUT OF SPACE

A Vanilla Custard with Fruit

Serves 4

Ingredients

2 cups milk

$\frac{1}{3}$ cup sugar

2 tablespoons cornstarch

2 eggs

1 teaspoon vanilla extract

1 banana

4 teaspoons maple syrup

Red and blue food coloring

Sweetworks Sixlets Shimmer Silver candies (optional)

Preparation

Whisk together the milk, sugar, and cornstarch in a medium saucepan over medium heat; allow bubbles at the edges of the mixture and whisk out clumps. Remove from heat.

In a medium bowl whisk the eggs and pour a portion of the milk mixture into the eggs slowly and continually whisk, and then reintroduce this back into the milk mixture. Keep whisking, at medium to low heat, increasing slowly to medium heat and allowing the mixture to thicken. Do not boil!

Add the extract and stir, allowing it to thicken further. Do not let the mixture cool.

Pour $\frac{1}{4}$ cup of the mixture into four small clear bowls and add three or four banana slices, $\frac{1}{2}$ teaspoon of maple syrup with a drop of red and blue food coloring.

Add another layer of custard ($\frac{1}{4}$ cup), banana, syrup, and food coloring, then top them off with the remaining custard. Sprinkle a dash of sugar on top with color and serve.

Place a piece of the silver candy on top if available.

THE CAKE IN YELLOW

Angel Food Cake
Serves 16

Ingredients

1½ cups powdered sugar

1 cup cake flour

12 egg whites, at room temperature

1½ teaspoons cream of tartar

1 cup sugar

1½ teaspoons vanilla

½ teaspoon almond extract

Yellow food coloring

¼ teaspoon salt

Various dipping sauces of your choosing

*The spirals
for 17 days
3 hours, 24 min

Each becomes 3*

Preparation

Move the oven rack to lowest position. Preheat the oven to 375°F.

In a medium bowl, mix together the powdered sugar and flour.

In a separate large bowl, whisk the egg whites and cream of tartar or use an electric mixer on medium speed until foamy. Then, on high speed, add the sugar, 2 tablespoons at a time.

Add the vanilla, almond extract, a few drops of food coloring, and salt before the last of the sugar is added. Beat until stiff and glossy peaks form.

Evenly sprinkle the sugar-flour mixture, ¼ cup at a time, over the meringue, folding it in just until the dry ingredients disappear.

Push the batter into an ungreased 10-by-4-inch angel food cake pan (tube pan).

Cut gently through the batter with a metal spatula to release air bubbles.

Bake for 30 minutes or until an inserted toothpick comes out dry
and top springs back when touched lightly.

Remove from the oven and immediately turn pan upside down onto heatproof
funnel or bottle. Let hang about 2 hours or until cake is completely cool.

Loosen the side of the cake with a knife or a long, metal spatula; remove from pan.

Cut the cake slowly with a serrated knife into 4-inch wedges and freeze the wedges.
Then cut them further into odd geometric shapes.

Serve with several dipping sauces of your choice.

THE RING THAT SHOULD NOT BE

Not Just Any Jell-O Mold

Serves 12

Ingredients

1 (15-ounce) can pear halves, reserve the syrup from the can

4 (3-ounce) packets unflavored gelatin

2 (6-ounce) boxes lime gelatin

1 (8-ounce) brick cream cheese

1 teaspoon citric acid

Yellow food coloring

3 tablespoons white sugar

Green food coloring

3 ounces rice noodles

Green sparkle gel icing, for topping

Gold luster dust, for topping

Silver luster dust, for topping

You will also need:

Squeeze bottle

Tentacle mold or round 8- or 9-inch cake pan

Ring mold

Preparation

Drain the pears and reserve their liquid. Put the pear halves into a
separate container and save for later in the recipe.

Take the pear liquid and measure it out. You should have just under $1\frac{1}{2}$ cups.
Add enough boiling water to bring it up to 2 cups and divide in half.

Put one cup of your reserved pear liquid into a small pot and sprinkle with two packets of
unflavored gelatin. Allow to bloom at room temperature for 10 minutes.

Once your unflavored gelatin is fully bloomed, add in 3 cups of boiling water
and both boxes of lime gelatin. Stir until all the gelatin is fully dissolved.

Over medium-low heat, add the cream cheese to the lime-pear gelatin mixture.

Stir continuously until all the cream cheese is melted. It should be a slightly thick,
creamy green liquid at this point.

Transfer the liquid from the above steps to an easy-to-manage
squeeze bottle and use it to fill the tentacle mold.

Pop the mold into the freezer for 15 minutes to quick chill and then transfer it
to the fridge for another 20 minutes to continue firming up (don't allow to
freeze completely, as the final product will be brittle rather than jiggly).

Remove the tentacle from the mold and transfer to an open-topped container in the fridge. Continue this process until you end up with the desired amount of tentacles (about 8 total).

Allow the tentacles to sit undisturbed in the open-air container overnight in the fridge to firm up even further.

Add the remaining pear liquid to a heat-safe bowl and sprinkle with the last two packets of unflavored gelatin and allow to bloom for 10 minutes.

Once bloomed, mix in 2 cups of boiling water, the citric acid, and enough yellow food coloring to bring the liquid to a bright gold color. Continue to stir until all the gelatin is fully dissolved.

Pour this mixture into the ring mold. It should only fill up the mold by about half.

Pop it into the fridge and allow to firm up for approximately 2 to 4 hours.

While the golden gelatin is setting, remelt the rest of the green gelatin from earlier, either on the stove over medium-low heat or in a microwave.

While it's melting, mash the pear halves from earlier and then add into the green gelatin mixture. Stir well to combine.

Pour 1 cup of this into a bowl roughly the size of the center of the ring mold and refrigerate until firm. Allow the rest of the green gelatin to cool to room temperature and then use to add a green layer to the underside of the golden ring layer in the ring mold.

Allow all the gelatin mixtures to now rest in the fridge and fully set.

In a small pot, bring 1 cup of water to a boil and add in the remaining 1 tablespoon white sugar, several drops of green food coloring, and the rice noodles. Cook until the noodles are tender and green. Drain and set aside for the final assembly.

To Assemble:

Fill a sink with hot water and briefly dunk the bottom of the ring mold until just slightly melted. Invert the mold over a plate or serving platter and de-mold.

Place a large handful of green rice noodles in the center of the ring mold and then arrange the tentacles out around the edge like the spokes of a wagon.

De-mold the smaller green gelatin from the bowl and place on top of the tentacles.

Drizzle the top of the green gelatin with green sparkle gel frosting and give the gelatin tentacles a light dusting of silver luster dust.

Lightly dust the golden pear section of your ring mold with gold luster dust for an added sparkle.

Serve chilled and enjoy both the light citrus and pear flavors and the unending screams of your chosen victims as they take in this unholy dessert.

ACKNOWLEDGMENTS

We must heap praise, gratitude, and veneration upon the following beloved cultists and contributors:

Annamarie Chestnut of Annnamarie's Restaurant in Royersford, Pennsylvania, kindly provided us the magnificent New England Damned Chowder.

Dave Maurer provided the Ahiä! Ahiä! Father Dagon! and The Fishes From Outside recipes, for which we are Deep Onely grateful. It's good to have chef friends.

Miguel Fliguer, author of the delectable *Cooking With Lovecraft* vouchsafed the Albino Penguin Au Vin Blanc.

Hellen Die, of the stygian and awesome *Eat The Dead Necro Nomnomnomicon* food blog provided two original recipes: Yogash the Gruel, and The Ring That Should Not Be.

Heather Hane of Stonybrook Meadery in Jim Thorpe, Pennsylvania, submitted Wilbur Whateley's Dunwich Sandwich. Strangely, it goes well with mead . . .

Deanna Visalle submitted the black delight of the Formless Spawnghetti, which remains a favorite in the author's house.

All else goes to family, Maggie Slater (the Unquestioned Mistress of the Kitchen, who let me live through this project despite that incident with the egg nog recipe . . .), my own dire experiments inspired by I dare not think what, and Tom Roache—Chief Culinary Executive Extraordinaire.

Lastly, but with infinite gratitude, we'd like to thank all of the initial backers that enabled us to ~~summon~~ create this work in the first place. Your enthusiasm, patience, input, and praise are all foundational ingredients here. We can't thank you enough.

We must also thank *Food & Wine* magazine, *Sy-Fy Wire*, Boardgamegeek.com, DreadCentral .com, and the many blogs and podcasts that noticed us and boosted the signal. The community we collectively create—is an awesome Thing to be part of. We are so grateful.

INDEX

Page numbers in italics indicate images.